Songs of Claude Debussy
Volume II: Medium Voice

A Critical Edition by James R. Briscoe

Based on primary sources, with commentary and translations.

Each song is presented in the original key.

On the cover: Claude Monet, *Water Lilies*, 1906, oil on canvas, 87.6 x 92.7 cm, Mr. and Mrs. Martin A. Ryerson Collection, 1933.1157, photograph © 1993 The Art Institute of Chicago. "You honor me greatly by calling me a student of Claude Monet." (Debussy to Émile Vuillermoz, 25 January 1916.)

Hal Leonard Publishing Corporation

7777 West Bluemound Road P.O. Box 13819 Milwaukee, WI 53213

JAMES R. BRISCOE is Professor in the Jordan College of Fine Arts at Butler University, where he teaches American, Classic, and Romantic music history. He compiled the *Historical Anthology of Music by Women* (Indiana University Press, 1987), and wrote the book *Claude Debussy: A Guide to Research* (Garland Publishing, New York, 1990). Previous Debussy editions include the unpublished songs *Sept Poèmes de Banville* (Paris: Jobert, 1985) and *Preludes for Piano, Books 1 and 2,* for G. Schirmer in 1991.

In the summer of 1990 he spoke at the International Musicological Society Symposium in Osaka, Japan, and at the International Franck Symposium in Belgium. Scholarly articles on women composers and on Debussy have appeared in 19th-Century Music, College Music Symposium, Musical Quarterly, Journal of Musicology, and Revue belge de musicologie.

Mr. Briscoe graduated with a bachelor's degree in cello from the University of Alabama, and with master's and doctorate degrees in musicology from the University of North Carolina. He received research and teaching grants from the French Government, Butler University, Indiana Humanities Council, National Endowment for the Humanities, Danforth Foundation, and Mellon Foundation. In 1984 Butler University students named him "Outstanding Teacher of the Year."

The editor expresses his appreciation to the following persons and institutions for generous permission to quote from their manuscripts in this edition:

      Mr. Georges Alphandéry, Montfavet, France
      Bibliothèque nationale, Paris, Département de la musique, Mme Catherine Massip, Directeur
      Mrs. Daniel Drachman
      Harvard University, the Houghton Library
      The Frederick R. Koch Foundation Collection,
            on deposit at the Pierpont Morgan LIbrary, New York
      The Carlton Lake Collection, Harry Ransom Humanities Research Center,
            The University of Texas at Austin
      Mme Françoise de Lastic, for the Collection Lang-Goüin,
            Abbaye de Royaumont, Asnières-sur-Oise, France
      Mr. Robert O. Lehman
      The Library of Congress, Music Division
      The Pierpont Morgan Library, Mr. J. Rigbie Turner, Curator of Music
      The Newberry Library, Chicago

The editor also thanks André Aerne, esteemed colleague and singer, for his review of this edition. It is dedicated with love to Madeleine and Rochelle, "un conseil de goûter le charme d'être au monde."

CONTENTS

listen
to

INTRODUCTION

The 85 art songs by Claude Debussy (1862-1918) span his entire creative output. His first compositions were songs, the earliest dating from about 1880, and his first publication was "Nuit d'étoiles" in 1882. Debussy as a composer was introduced to the public that year, when as pianist he joined his benefactor Marie-Blanche Vasnier for the premier of "Fête galante," included in the present collection. In the ensuing years through1887, 46 songs were written. Many of these were for the light but versatile soprano voice of Madame Vasnier, "a melodious fairy voice," as Debussy expressed it. She was a beautiful woman of the haute bourgeoisie and an accomplished singer, highly esteemed by critics; her husband Eugène guided Debussy toward contemporary literature and the other arts. The financial, artistic, and intellectual support of the Vasniers enabled the young composer to evolve beyond the conservative artistic boundaries of the Paris Conservatoire. That is perhaps why the genre of song first shows the technical innovations and the new sensibilities toward literature that he would cultivate in his mature work, which set a pace for twentieth century music. However reluctantly, the young Debussy nonetheless conformed to the musical establishment and wrote the required cantatas and choral works for the Conservatoire, climaxing in the Prix de Rome cantata *L'enfant prodigue* of 1884. The poets Paul Bourget and Théodore de Banville are literary preoccupations of Debussy in his early songs to about 1886. Banville especially parallels Debussy's and the Symbolists' value of artistic suggestion over outright statement, "of things said in part." Alongside Banville, the Symbolists Verlaine, in the early Fêtes galantes pour Madame Vasnier and the Ariettes oubliées, and Mallarmé, in "Apparition," make their first appearance.

From 1887 to 1915, when he composed his last song "Noël des enfants qui n'ont plus de maisons," Debussy completed 39 songs. More than any other artistic trend, Symbolism dominates the aesthetic of Debussy, whereby he remains faithful to the realm of the dream, the illusion, and the fantasy. Debussy is unified with the Symbolists in the artistic desire, as Stefan Jarocinski noted, "to use the free interplay of resemblances, associations, of far-off echos… an open form capable of receiving various meanings without having any definite meaning in itself." In his maturity Debussy includes his own texts among those by Charles Baudelaire, Tristan Lhermite, and Pierre Louÿs, all in the Symbolist realm. After 1898, however, he found inspiration of a noble, gentle, but also nationalistic sort in earlier French poetry by Charles d'Orléans and François Villon. This classicicizing tendency was also to increase in the instrumental compositions of later maturity. Altogether, Debussy set the writings of 23 poets as art songs.

NOTES ON THE EDITION

This edition presents 62 of Debussy's songs in two volumes, and it includes the one aria from the cantata *L'enfant prodigue* that figures in the modern recital repertory. All of the songs Debussy chose to publish are included, as are the choicest of the early songs published posthumously. Furthermore, the early version of Fantoches is presented for the first time. Certain of the omitted songs have not been recovered or are inaccessible in private collections. The other songs not included, just as the inaccessible ones, date from Debussy's youth. In some cases, inexperience and the need to follow existing idioms result in songs of perhaps a lesser interest for the repertory. In the volume for high voice, the high range with occasional emphasis on the middle tessitura predominates. It seems that the voice type of Marie-Blanche Vasnier, which domintated the youthful song writing, continued to exert its effect for some years after Debussy stopped writing specifically for her. Moreover, a generally late-Romantic melodic idiom prevailed. The volume for medium voice contains the songs of maturity, in which a middle voice range seemed appropriate to Debussy for his typically Symbolist understatement.

Sources

Two types of primary sources are considered basic to this edition: autograph manuscripts and first editions supervised by Debussy. The primary sources that were consulted are indicated in the notes following each song. In every case, the edition on legal deposit at the Bibliothèque nationale in Paris was consulted as the first edition, and the autograph manuscripts listed were consulted directly.

Editorial Procedure

When there is a variant reading among sources, that of the first edition is generally preferred. Debussy probably emended the autograph reading in the publisher's proofs, or else he revised the song in an autograph manuscript not recovered. In any case, it is presumed that the first edition usually represents the composer's final intent. When a song was published posthumously and thus not under Debussy's supervision, the autograph is generally preferred in the event of variant readings.

Notes list the primary sources considered and indicate further details of the composition. Numbered notes refer to the sources and describe all significant variant readings among primary sources. This edition resolves minor variants without further note, such as missing accidentals confirmed in another voice and stem directions. In every case, this edition signals all variants among sources and editorial departures from the primary sources of any musical significance, whether by numbered notes or by placing editorial insertions in brackets.

This edition brings stem direction and the notation of rests into conformity with modern practice. It adopts without further comment the current preference for beaming eighth notes and smaller values in voice lines instead of the traditional flagged notes for separate syllables. In the present case, the division of syllables in the French underlay is clarified by hyphens consistently. Final, unaccented e's in French words customarily are not spoken but are sung in music. Often but not consistently in Debussy's autograph manuscripts and first editions, the final tone setting the e was joined to the penultimate tone by a tie. Current practice discourages such ties into final e's. In the present edition, they are eliminated except when an actual slur is in question. The primary sources were also inconsistent in slurs indicating phrases: here, the slur is extended to cover such final syllables without further editorial comment. Traditional French notation in the primary sources occasionally spread a chord in one hand over both treble and bass clefs; the current edition notates a chord in its entirety within the appropriate clef, using leger lines and making no further comment editorially. In no case, however, is a polyphonic line in the accompaniment obscured or is any pitch or duration altered. The indication of such terms as crescendo and accelerando, which the primary sources hyphenate and spread across several measures on occasion, herein is stated simply at once. Such instructions are understood to continue until another instruction takes over. The indications "Tempo I°" and "I° Tempo" are standardized as the former term. Internal double bars, except when they indicate a major structural division, are reduced to single barlines according to modern practice.

Dedications are those indicated in the first edition or, in the case of posthumous editons, in the manuscript.

Dates given beneath each song title refer to the date of composition, which sometimes precedes publication by some time.

Capitalization and punctuation in the French text underlay follows that of the original poem, as does spelling. Debussy's orthographic errors in the autograph manuscripts are corrected without further mention. However, his deliberate modifications of the poem are retained, and a numbered note signals the original text of the poem.

Translations into English are by the editor and seek a compromise between a literal but awkward translation, and an elegant but too often remote one. To assist performers, the translations are given alongside the French text. The translations proceed line for line and maintain the punctuation that ends each line of the French.

Abbreviations

A- among sources, signifies an autograph manuscript

E-signifies the first edition of a song

EP-signifies the first posthumous edition

l.h. -left hand; also m.g., main gauche

r.h.-right hand; also m.d., main droite

[ ]-Brackets indicate an interpolation by the editor of a detail not found in the primary sources. Note that parentheses are used only when they occur in the primary sources, such as for reminder accidentals.

NOTES AND TRANSLATIONS

Deux romances

I. Romance: L'âme évaporée
(The soul evanescent)

L'âme évaporée et soufrante,	*The soul evanescent and suffering,*
L'âme douce, l'âme odorante	*The sweet soul, the soul fragrant*
Des lys divins que j'ai cueillis	*With divine lilies that I gathered*
Dans le jardin de ta pensée,	*In the garden of your thought,*
Où donc les vents l'ont-ils chassée,	*Where have the winds driven it away,*
Cette âme adorable des lys?	*This adorable soul of the lilies?*
N'est-il plus un parfum qui reste	*Is there no longer a scent remaining*
De la suavité céleste	*Of the celestial softness*
Des jours où tu m'enveloppais	*Of those days when you enveloped me*
D'une vapeur surnaturelle,	*In an otherworldly vapor*
Faite d'espoir, d'amour fidèle,	*Made of hope, of true love,*
De béatitude et de paix?	*Of beauty and peace?*

Notes for the set *Deux romances*

SOURCES
A: Paris, Bibliothèque nationale, manuscrit 995. Source A contains the date 1891, but it appears to be a fair copy prepared for publication that year. The style of *Deux romances* suggests the earlier composition date of about 1885-86.
E: Paris: Durand et Schoenewerk, 1891.
"Romance—L'âme évaporée" was reissued by Durand in 1907, and "Les cloches" in 1906. Both contain few revisions except for the addition of an English text beneath the French.

Notes for "Romance: L'âme évaporée"

1. The optional notes in the voice occur in both A and E.

II. Les cloches
(The Bells)

Les feuilles s'ouvraient sur le bord des branches,	*The leaves opened along the sides of the branches,*
Délicatement,	*Delicately,*
Les cloches tintaient, légères et franches,	*The bells pealed, light and clear,*
Dans le ciel clément.	*In the mild sky.*
Rythmique et fervent comme une antienne,	*Rhythmic and fervent as an antiphon,*
Ce lointain appel	*That distant peal*
Me remémorait la blancheur chrétienne	*Brought to mind the Christian purity*
Des fleurs de l'autel.	*Of altar flowers.*
Ces cloches parlaient d'heureuses années,	*Those bells spoke of happy years,*
Et, dans le grand bois,	*And, throughout the vast woods,*
Semblaient reverdir les feuilles fanées	*Seemed again to turn green the withered leaves*
Des jours d'autrefois.	*Of days gone by.*

Sources are indicated above for the set.

1. The title of Bourget's poem is "Romance." Source A contains no title; E gives "Les cloches."
2. A and E: *meno cresc.*; the 1906 reissue as printed.
3. A adds a sharp to b^1 in r.h. , m. 13, apparently in error; E as printed.

Les angélus
(The Angelus)

Cloches chrétiennes pour les matines,	*Christian bells for morning prayer,*
Sonnant au cœur d'espérer encore!	*Calling for the heart to hope still!*
Angélus angélisés d'aurore!	*Angelus bells made angelic by the dawn!*
Las! où sont vos prières câlines?	*Alas! where are your comforting prayers?*
Vous étiez de si douces folies!	*You sang of such gentle follies!*
Et chanterelles d'amour prochaines!	*And the high bells of coming love!*
Aujourd'hui souveraine est ma peine,	*Today my sorrow is sovereign,*
Et toutes matines abolies.	*And morning prayers are no more.*
Je ne vis plus que d'ombre et de soir;	*I see nothing save shadow and evening;*
Les las angélus pleurent la mort,	*The weary Angelus laments the dead,*
Et là, dans mon cœur résigné, dort	*And there, in my resigned heart, sleeps*
La seule veuve de tout espoir.	*The lonely widow of all hope.*

SOURCES
A: in an inaccessible private collection in the United States
E: Paris: Hamelle, 1891

Trois mélodies de Paul Verlaine
(Three songs on poems by Verlaine)

I. La mer est plus belle
(The sea is more beautiful)

La mer est plus belle	*The sea is more beautiful*
Que les cathédrales,	*Than cathedrals,*
Nourrice fidèle,	*Faithful nurse,*
Berceuse de râles,	*Cradle of the rail birds,*
La mer sur qui prie	*The sea over which prays*
La Vierge Marie!	*The Virgin Mary!*
Elle a tous les dons	*It possesses all qualities*
Terribles et doux.	*Terrible and gentle.*
J'entends ses pardons	*I hear its pardons*
Gronder ses courroux.	*And the roar of its anger.*
Cette immensité	*This immense power*
N'a rien d'entêté.	*Has no willful intent.*
Oh! si patiente,	*Oh! so patient,*
Même quand méchante!	*Even when wicked!*
Un souffle ami hante	*A friendly breath haunts*
La vague, et nous chante:	*The wave, and sings to us:*
"Vous sans espérance,	*"You who are without hope,*
Mourez sans souffrance!"	*May you die without suffering!"*

La mer est plus belle, continued

Et puis, sous les cieux	*And then, beneath the skies*
Qui s'y rient plus clairs,	*That sport about more brightly,*
Elle a des airs bleus,	*It appears blue,*
Roses, gris et verts…	*Pink, gray and green…*
Plus belle que tous,	*More beautiful than all things,*
Meilleure que nous!	*Better than we!*

Notes for *Trois Mélodies de Paul Verlaine*

Songs 2 and 3 are dated to 1891 by a letter from Debussy to Robert Godet, dated January 30, 1892: "I have written two *mélodies*… They are dedicated to you." Debussy submitted them for publication a full ten years later. In that edition, song 1 is dedicated to Ernest Chausson, while songs 2 and 3 are dedicated to Robert Godet, as printed.

SOURCES
A: Paris, Bibliothèque nationale, manuscrit 20633. The text underlay is rewritten in an an unidentified hand, and the autograph contains indications by the engraver and by the publisher Hamelle.
E: Paris: Hamelle, 1901

Notes for "La mer est plus belle"

1. A: *dim.* not at m. 9 but at m. 10, and in rh. no e-sharp1 m. 10 or d-sharp[1] m.11. E as printed.
2. A: no natural to *a* or *a*[1], m. 23-24; E as printed and required harmonically.
3. A, vocal line m. 36-40:

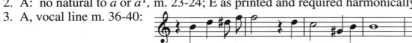

A, m. 39 l.h. upper line: b (♩), e[1] (♩), g[1] [sharp] (♩) tied to g[1] (♩) m. 40. E as printed.

II. Le son du cor
(The sound of the horn)

Le son du cor s'afflige vers les bois	*The sound of the horn goes grieving in the woods*
D'une douleur on veut croire orpheline	*With a sadness that one would think orphan-like [,]*
Qui vient mourir au bas de la colline	*A sound that has died away at the foot of the hill*
Parmi la bise errant en courts abois.	*Amidst the stirring north wind with its short howls.*
L'âme du loup pleure dans cette voix	*The soul of the wolf weeps in that voice*
Qui monte avec le soleil qui décline	*That rises as the sun sets*
D'une agonie on veut croire câline	*In an agony one would find soothing*
Et qui ravit et qui navre à la fois.	*And that both enchants and distresses us.*
Pour faire mieux cette plainte assoupie,	*To enhance this subtle lament,*
La neige tombe à longs traits de charpie	*Snow is falling in long strands of rag*
A travers le couchant sanguinolent,	*Before the blood-red sunset,*
Et l'air à l'air d'être un soupir d'automne,	*And the air appears as an autumn sigh,*
Tant il fait doux par ce soir monotone	*So quiet is this monotonous evening*
Où se dorlote un paysage lent.	*By which the sluggish landscape is humored.*

Sources are indicated above for the set.

1. A, m. 2 r.h.:

E:

The present notation clarifies the r.h. rhythm that Debussy apparently intended.

Le son du cor, continued

2. A, m. 19-20 l.h.: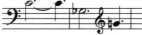

3. A sustains the final d-natural of m. 28, in the voice, through m. 29, beat 1.

III. L'échelonnement des haies
(The expanse of the hedgerows)

L'échelonnement des haies	*The expanse of the hedgerows*
Moutonne à l'infini, mer	*Billows infinitely,*
Claire dans le brouillard clair	*A clear sea in the light mist*
Qui sent bon les jeunes baies.	*Fragrant with young berries.*
Des arbres et des moulins	*Trees and mills*
Sont légers sur le vert tendre	*Are set against the delicate green*
Où vient s'ébattre et s'étendre	*Where to gambol and frisk*
L'agilité des poulains.	*The young colts come.*
Dans ce vague d'un Dimanche	*In this Sunday dreaminess*
Voici se jouer aussi	*Here also are playing about*
De grandes brebis aussi	*Heavy ewes, as*
Douces que leur laine blanche.	*Soft as their white wool.*
Tout à l'heure déferlait	*Just now there rolled out*
L'onde roulée en volutes,	*In a wave, unfurled like a scroll,*
De cloches comme des flûtes	*Bells like flutes*
Dans le ciel comme du lait.	*In the milk-white sky.*

Sources are indicated above for the set.

1. A, rhythm in voice m. 5-6:

2. A: no *p* m. 8
3. A: no c-natural^1, m. 19 l.h. beats 2 and 4, and no inner line c^1/b-flat/d^1 in l.h. m. 20 beats 2-4. Source A extends the voice line into m. 21, ending on a-flat^1 for the syllable "-che."
4. A: no sharp to *a* in l.h.; that in E (printed) is necessary to the succeeding cadence on B.

Fêtes galantes, série I

I. En sourdine
(Muted)

Calmes dans le demi-jour	*Calm in the half-light*
Que les branches hautes font,	*That the high branches make,*
Pénétrons bien notre amour	*Let us permeate our love*
De ce silence profond.	*With this profound silence.*
Fondons nos âmes, nos cœurs	*Let us melt together our souls, our hearts*
Et nos sens extasiés,	*And our senses in ecstasy,*
Parmis les vagues langueurs	*Among the vague languors*
Des pins et des arbousiers.	*Of the pines and arbutus trees.*
Ferme tes yeux à demi,	*Half close your eyes,*
Croise tes bras sur ton sein,	*Fold your arms on your breast,*
Et de ton cœur endormi	*And from your sleeping heart*
Chasse à jamais tout dessein.	*Drive away all care forever.*

En sourdine, continued

Laissons-nous persuader	*Let us be drawn*
Au souffle berceur et doux,	*By the gentle, rocking wind,*
Qui vient à tes pieds rider	*That comes to ripple at your feet*
Les ondes de gazon roux.	*The waves of russet grass.*
Et quand, solennel, le soir	*And when solemnly the evening*
Des chênes noirs tombera,	*Shall fall from the dark oaks,*
Voix de notre désespoir,	*That voice of our despair,*
Le rossignol chantera.	*The nightingale will sing.*

Notes on the set *Fêtes galantes I*

The phrase "Fête galante" is not readily translated. "Courtly outing" as preferred in the body of the translation conveys the sense of an 18th-century excursion by the upper classes in gardens or gentle woods. Both Verlaine and Debussy referred to the Rococo court painter Watteau, who specialized in such scenes but imbued them with mystery and even foreboding.

All three songs of *Fêtes galantes I* exist in early versions and are presented in Volume I (for High Voice) of this edition.

SOURCES

A1: Collection of Robert Lehman, formerly Denise Jobert-Georges

The autographs of "Clair de lune" and "Fantoches" contain markings that indicate they served as fair copies for the publisher. The order of A1 is "En sourdine," "Clair de lune," and "Fantoches." The present order reflects that of source E. In source A1, a dedication appears only for "Clair de lune," "à Madame A. Fontaine." No dates appear on the copy made available to this edition, although Lesure (1977) and Cobb (1982) report the date 1891.

A2: Song 1 only, "En sourdine," at the Carlton Lake Collection, Harry Ransom Humanities Research Center, University of Texas, Austin. Dated "Mai [18]92" and dedicated to Catherine Stevens, with whom Debussy was romantically involved at the time: "à Mademoiselle Catherine Stevens en Hommage, et pour marquer un peu de ma joie d'être son affectueusement dévoué, C. A. Debussy" ["To Miss Catherine Stevens in homage, and to show a measure of my joy in being her affectionately devoted C.A. Debussy"].

E: Paris: Fromont, 1903.

The dedications appearing in E are retained, although the dates of composition given here are those of sources A1 and A2.

Notes for "En sourdine"

1. A1 differs substantially from A2 and E where "En sourdine" is concerned, and A1 relates more to the 1882 version. A2 is closer to E, but was revised prior to publication. Since no publisher's proofs leading to E are traced, E remains the basic source. Indications of dynamics vary frequently, and those of E are retained without further remark except as noted below.
2. A1: *Très lent*, suggesting that the "Rêveusement lent" of A2 and E is a rather slow tempo. Perhaps *tempo rubato* also is implied. A2 but not E: tenuto to bass chords m. 1-3.
3. M. 4, E as printed; A2 indicates in the piano:

4. A2 but not E: *plus p*; *più* is editorial translation for consistency of language. A2: *Toujours plus doux* m. 9.
5. A2 sustains the low bass D-sharp/A-sharp of m. 9 through m. 10.
6. E, r.h. upper voice: ♩ , followed by ♫ . A2: ♩. followed by ♫ . Both are inaccurate, and the present solution appears to be Debussy's intent. A2, m. 14: *1er mouvt.*, followed by *un peu retenu* m. 15; E as printed. E but not A2 m. 18: *En animant un peu*.

En sourdine, continued

7. A2, voice, m. 20-31 differ from E, as does the piano part in small detail; E is retained.
8. A2: *Plus lent*; E: *Intimement doux*. At m. 29, A2 but not E: *Animé*.
9. E: *Un peu plus lent*, clarified by the indication *1er Mouvt.* [*A tempo*] of A2. E, the upper line of the piano m. 32: ♪♩. ♪ A2 as printed. The lower voices of the piano, source A, are different; those of E are retained.
10. A2 and E incorrectly double-dot the first notes in the piano, m. 33-34 and 40-41.

II. Fantoches
(Marionettes)

Scaramouche et Pulcinella	*Scaramouche and Pulcinella*
Qu'un mauvais dessein rassembla	*Whom some evil scheme brought together*
Gesticulent, noirs sous la lune.	*Gesticulate, black figures beneath the moon.*
Cependant l'excellent docteur	*Meanwhile, the fine doctor*
Bolonais cueille avec lenteur	*From Bologna slowly gathers*
Des simples parmi l'herbe brune.	*Simples among the dark grass.*
Lors sa fille, piquant minois,	*Then his daughter, that saucy looker,*
Sous la charmille, en tapinois,	*Beneath the bower slyly*
Se glisse demi-nue en quête	*Slips in, half nude, in quest*
De son beau pirate espagnol,	*Of her handsome Spanish pirate,*
Dont un amoureux rossignol	*Whose distress an amorous nightingale*
Clame la détresse à tue-tête.	*Proclaims in full voice.*

Notes on the text
        Scaramouche and Pulcinella are comic figures appearing in the traveling street theatre of 18th-century Italy, the Commedia dell'arte. The "doctor from Bologna" might be Pantaloon, Columbine's father. "Simples" are herbs used for medicine.

Sources are indicated above for the set.

General Note: Certain aspects of dynamics and articulation are not present in A1 but are found in E, added probably at the proof stage. These are included here.

1. E, rhythm in voice: ♪♪♪♩ ; A1 as printed, analogous to m. 9 and 24.

2. A1 repeats the text "Gesticulent…lune" and gives a melisma on "lu-" of the second "lune." The Verlaine poem gives "langoureux" instead of Deubssy's "amoureux rossignol." E as printed.
3. A1 but not E: *cresc. - decresc.* m. 37-39.
4. A1 concludes the vocal line at the present m. 60, followed by a rather simplistic postlude of 10 measures. E as printed. The text "la" does not occur in the Verlaine poem.

III. Clair de lune
(Moonlight)

Votre âme est un paysage choisi	*Your soul is a choice landscape*
Que vont charmants masques et bergamasques	*Where charming maskers and bergamaskers go about*
Jouant du luth et dansant et quasi	*Playing the lute and dancing and are almost*
Tristes sous leurs déguisements fantasques.	*Sad beneath their whimsical disguises.*
Tout en chantant sur le mode mineur	*While singing in the minor of*
L'amour vainqueur et la vie opportune,	*Love triumphant and the good life,*
Ils n'ont pas l'air de croire à leur bonheur	*They seem not to believe in their own happiness*
Et leur chanson se mêle au clair de lune,	*And their song is mixed and lost in the moonlight.*

Clair de lune, continued

Au calme clair de lune triste et beau,	*In the calm moonlight, sad and beautiful,*
Qui fait rêver les oiseaux dans les arbres	*That makes the birds dream in the trees*
Et sangloter d'extase les jets d'eau,	*And the fountains sob in ecstasy,*
Les grands jets d'eau sveltes parmi les marbres.	*Those tall, slender fountains among the statues.*

Sources are indicated above for the set.

1. A1: *Andantino*; E as printed. A1: no prelude of 4 m. as in source E (printed). A1 begins at printed m. 5, but without low bass GG-sharp. Other revisions of A1 that were made for E are at m. 7, 13-16, 30-31, and in minor details elsewhere. These revisions contribute a more supple setting of the Verlaine and a closer mirror of its spirit in the piano.
2. E: no *cresc.-decresc.* m. 10-11; A1 as printed.
3. E: ♩. beat 2, first f-sharp^2 incorrectly given as g-sharp^2. A as printed. In m. 23 previously, both A1 and E give DD-sharp in the low bass, downbeat. Considering the prevailing 2-measure pattern, that seems a lapse of Debussy's concentration, and FF-sharp is given here paralleling m. 24.
4. A1 and E m. 26: flat to f^1 in l.h., but natural to f^2 in r.h. and voice.
5. E: sharp to e^2 in voice, as printed, A1: no sharp.

Proses lyriques
(Lyric Prose-Poems)

I. De rêve
(Of dreaming)

La nuit a des douceurs de femme!	*The night has a woman's sweetness!*
Et les vieux arbres sous la lune d'or, songent!	*And the old trees beneath the golden moon, dream*
A celle qui vient de passer la tête emperlée,	*Of her who has just passed, her head adorned with pearls,*
Maintenant navrée,	*Heartbroken now!*
À jamais navrée,	*Forever heartbroken!*
Ils n'ont pas su lui faire signe…	*They knew not how to signal her…*
Toutes! Elles ont passé	*All of them! All have passed*
Les Frêles,	*The frail women,*
Les Folles,	*The foolish,*
Semant leur rire au gazon grêle,	*Sowing their laughter on the sparse grass,*
Aux brises frôleuses la caresse charmeuse	*In the soft breezes the charming allure*
Des hanches fleurissantes!	*Of their florid hips!*
Hélas! de tout ceci, plus rien qu'un blanc frisson.*Alas!*	*Of all this, nothing remains save a pale shudder.*
Les vieux arbres sous la lune d'or pleurent	*The old trees beneath the golden moon, weep for*
Leurs belles feuilles d'or,	*Their beautiful golden leaves*
Nul ne leur dédiera plus la fierté des casques d'or	*No one will grant them the pride of golden helmets*
Maintenant ternis,	*Tarnished now!*
À jamais ternis. Les chevaliers sont morts	*Forever tarnished! The knights have died*
sur le chemin du Grâal!	* in search of the Grail!*
La nuit a des douceurs de femmes!	*The night has the sweetness of women!*
Des mains semblent frôler les âmes	*Certain hands seem to caress souls*
Mains si folles, si frêles,	*Hands so foolish, so frail,*
Au temps où les épées chantaient pour Elles!…	*In the time when swords sang their valiant song for Them!…*
D'étranges soupirs s'élèvent sous les arbres.	*Strange sighs rise up from under the trees.*
Mon âme! c'est du rêve ancien qui t'étreint!	*My soul! It is some ancient dream that grips you!*

SOURCES
A: inaccessible private collection in France
E: Paris: Fromont, 1895
     Debussy's prose-poem "De rêve" appeared in *Entretiens politiques et littéraires* (Paris) in Dec. 1892, p. 269-270. For source E, Debussy changed certain words, capitalization, and punctuation, which are retained.

14

II. De grève
(Of shores)

Sur la mer les crépuscules tombent,	*On the sea the twilights fall,*
Soie blanche effilée!	*White, frayed silk!*
Les vagues comme de petites folles,	*Waves like giddy girls,*
Jasent, petites filles sortant de l'école,	*They chatter, young girls leaving school,*
Parmi les froufrous de leur robe,	*Among the swishing of their dress,*
Soie verte irisée!	*Green iridescent silk!*
Les nuages, graves voyageurs,	*Clouds, serious voyagers,*
Se concertent sur le prochain orage,	*Plot out the coming storm,*
Et, c'est un fond vraiment trop grave	*And, it is a background truly too dark*
À cette anglaise aquarelle.	*For this English watercolor.*
Les vagues, les petites vagues,	*The waves, the little waves,*
Ne savent plus où se mettre,	*No longer know where to turn,*
Car voici la méchante averse,	*For here comes a nasty shower,*
Froufrous de jupes envolées,	*Swishing of skirts in the air,*
Soie verte affolée.	*Bewildered green silk.*
Mais la lune, compatissante à tous!	*But the moon, sympathetic to all!*
Vient apaiser ce gris conflit,	*Comes out to clam this gray conflict,*
Et caresse lentement ses petites amies,	*And slowly soothes his little friends,*
Qui s'offrent comme lèvres aimantes	*Who offer themselves, like loving lips*
À ce tiède et blanc baiser.	*To this warm and white kiss.*
Puis, Plus rien!	*Nothing, nothing more!*
Plus que les cloches attardées	*Nothing save the belated bells*
Des flottantes églises	*Of floating churches*
Angélus des vagues,	*Angelus of the waves,*
Soie blanche apaisée!	*Becalmed white silk!*

SOURCES
A: not located
E: Paris: Fromont, 1895
   Debussy's prose-poem "De grève" appeared in *Entretiens politiques et littéraires* (Paris) in Dec. 1892, p. 270-271.

III. De fleurs
(Of flowers)

Dans l'ennui si désolément vert	*In the boredom so desolately green*
De la serre de douleur,	*Of the hothouse of sorrow,*
Des Fleurs enlacent mon cœur	*Flowers entwine my heart*
De leurs tiges méchantes.	*In their cruel tendrils.*
Ah! quand reviendront autour de ma tête	*Ah! when will they come and surround my head again*
Les chères mains si tendrement désenlaceuses?	*Those dear hands so tenderly soothing?*
Les grands Iris violets	*The great violet irises*
Violèrent méchamment tes yeux,	*Ravage your eyes violently,*
En semblant les refléter,	*While pretending to reflect them,*
Eux, qui furent l'eau du songe	*They who were the water of the dream*
Où plongèrent mes rêves si doucement	*Into which my dreams plunged so gently*
Enclos en leur couleur;	*Dreams enclosed by their color;*
Et les lys, blancs jets d'eau de pistils embaumés,	*And the lilies, white fountains smelling of pistils,*
Ont perdu leur grâce blanche	*Have lost their pale grace*
Et ne sont plus que pauvres malades sans soleil!	*And are now only poor invalids without the sun!*

De fleurs, continued

Soleil! ami des fleurs mauvaises,	*Sun! friend of evil flowers,*
Tueur de rêves! Tueur d'illusions	*Killer of dreams! Killer of illusions*
Ce pain béni des âmes misérables!	*The blessed bread of miserable souls!*
Venez! Venez! Les mains salvatrices!	*Come! Come! Hands of salvation!*
Brisez les vitres de mensonge,	*Shatter the panes of delusion,*
Brisez les vitres de maléfice,	*Shatter the panes of evil,*
Mon âme meurt de trop de soleil!	*My soul dies from too much sun!*
Mirages! Plus ne refleurira la joie de mes yeux,	*Mirages! No more will joy in my eyes be reflected,*
Et mes mains sont lasses de prier,	*And my hands are weary from praying,*
Mes yeux sont las de pleurer!	*My eyes are weary from weeping!*
Eternellement ce bruit fou	*Eternally this mad sound*
Des pétales noirs de l'ennui,	*Of petals that are black with boredom,*
Tombant goutte à goutte sur ma tête	*Falling drop by drop on my head*
Dans le vert de la serre de douleur!	*In the greenness of the hothouse of sorrow!*

SOURCES for "De fleurs" and "De soir"
A: Paris, Bibliothèque nationale, manuscrit 8642 contains both "De fleurs" and "De soir" and is titled "1er Cahier de proses lyriques… proses 3, 4." The dedication reads: "à Madame M. A. Fontaine, en hommage à sa voix si délicieusement musicienne. Claude Debussy" ["to Madame M.A. Fontaine, in homage to her voice, so delightfully musical, CD"]. Source A differs from source E in a number of details; major variants are noted, while in the case of minor ones source E is repeated without remark.

A further manuscript exists in an Austrian private collection, bearing the date June 1893 and the dedication "à Madame E. Chausson pour sa fête, et pour rendre respectueusement hommage au charme qu'elle met à être Madame Chausson" [reported in M. Cobb, 1982]. It was not accessible but would appear to be an earlier version than source A.

E: Paris: Fromont, 1895
The dedications found in E are retained here.

1. A but not E: *Rit.*
2. A, upper voice of l.h.: at m. 23, triplets on beat 2 are c, f, c; at. m. 25, triplets on beat 2 are e, a, e; at m. 26, beats 2-4, c-natural a c, a c a, c a c. E as printed.
3. A omits low bass F-sharp/FF-sharp at m. 32, tied from m. 31. M. 38, r.h. beat 3: E gives e-sharp^2 in lower voice, 2nd eighth-note value. A as printed, d-sharp2.
4. A does not include the m. 50 of source E (printed). Instead, A places the syllables "-ra-bles!" ($\quad$) over the accompaniment of the present m. 51-52.
5. A repeats the 2 r.h. chords m. 55 beat 4 at m. 56 beat 2; E as printed.
6. Source A delays the text "Mirages" to m. 65. A has lined through a first version, which gave the rhythm (m. 64-65):

7. E: no fermata or rest in vocal line; A as printed.

IV. De soir
(Of evening)

Dimanche sur les villes,	*Sunday over cities,*
Dimanche dans les cœurs!	*Sunday in hearts!*
Dimanche chez les petites filles	*Sunday for little girls*
Chantant d'une voix informée	*Who sing in a knowing voice*
Des rondes obstinées	*Persistent rounds*
Ou de bonnes Tours	*About how fine Towers*
N'en ont plus que pour quelques jours!	*Have only a few days remaining to them!*

De soir, continued

Dimanche, les gares sont folles!
Tout le monde appareille
Pour des banlieues d'aventure
En se disant adieu
Avec des gestes éperdus!

Dimanche les trains vont vite,
Dévorés par d'insatiables tunnels;
Et les bons signaux des routes
Échangent d'un œil unique
Des impressions toutes mécaniques.

Dimanche, dans le bleu de mes rêves
Où mes pensées tristes
De feux d'artifices manqués
Ne veulent plus quitter
Le deuil de vieux Dimanches trépassés.

Et la nuit à pas de velours
Vient endormir le beau ciel fatigué
Et c'est Dimanche dans les avenues d'étoiles;
La Vierge or sur argent
Laisse tomber les fleurs de sommeil!

Vite, les petits anges
Dépassez les hirondelles
Afin de vous coucher
Forts d'absolution!
Prenez pitié des villes,
Prenez pitié des cœurs,
Vous, la Vierge or sur argent!

Sunday, the train stations are wild!
Everyone prepares
For the suburbs of adventure
Bidding farewell to each other
With bewildered gestures!

Sunday the trains go quickly,
Devoured by insatiable tunnels;
And the kindly railroad signals
Share with their single eye
Mechanical observations.

Sunday, in the blue of my dreams
Where my sad thoughts
Of failed fireworks
No longer wish to abandon
The grief of old Sundays dead and gone.

And the night on velvet footsteps
Comes to send off to sleep the lovely tired sky,
And it is Sunday on the avenues of the stars;
The Virgin of gold on silver
Lets fall the flowers of sleep!

Quickly, little angels
Fly past the swallows
So that you may sleep
Strong in absolution!
Take pity on the cities,
Take pity on the hearts,
You, Virgin of gold on silver!

SOURCES: see above, for "De fleurs"

In addition, an early draft of "De soir" is Paris, Bibliothèque nationale, manuscrit 19183, containing the date "à la fin juin [18]93." Ms. 19183 is dedicated to Mme. Ernest Chausson, although source E dedicates "De soir" to Henry Lerolle. As for each of the *Proses Lyriques* in the present edition, the dedication of source E is retained.

1. A but not E includes *a,* beat 3 l.h.
2. A: no *sfz* m. 31-32; A gives *più f* m. 34. E as printed both places.
3. A, rhythm in voice:

E, m. 39: no natural to a^2 and a^1; A as printed, analogous to m. 36 and m. 39-40.
4. A: m. 48 beat 4, l.h. triplets: d-flat^1, b-flat, f; E as printed.
5. A but not E: *un peu retenu;* E m. 57: d-sharp^2 instead of rest in r.h. upper line; A as printed.
6. A: rhythm in voice on "Vier-ge": E as printed.

7. A: rhythm in r.h. m. 103: E as printed. A does not include the present m. 106 and 108, which are found in E.

Trois chansons de Bilitis
(Three Songs of Bilitis)

I. La flûte de Pan
(Pan's pipe)

Pour le jour des Hyacinthies, il m'a donné une syrinx faite
de roseaux bien taillés, unis avec la blanche cire qui est
as
douce à mes lévres comme le miel.

*For Hyacinthus's day, he gave me a panpipe made
of carefully assembled reeds, joined with a white wax that is*

sweet to my lips as honey.

Il m'apprend à jouer, assise sur ses genoux; mais je suis un
peu tremblante. Il en joue après moi, si doucement que je
l'entends à peine.

*He teaches me to play, seated in his lap, but I am a
little fearful. He plays it after me, so softly that I
can hardly hear him.*

Nous n'avons rien à nous dire, tant nous sommes près l'un
de l'autre; mais nos chansons veulent se répondre, et tour à
tour nos bouches s'unissent sur la flûte.

*We have nothing to say to each other, so close are we to each
other; but our songs try to answer each other, and little by
little our mouths join on the flute.*

Il est tard; voici le chant des grenouilles vertes qui
commence avec la nuit. Ma mère ne croira jamais que je
suis restée si longtemps à chercher ma ceinture perdue.

*It is late; there is the song of the green frogs that
begins at nightfall. My mother will never believe that I
stayed so long just looking for my lost sash.*

Notes on the text
    Pan was the Greek god of shepherds and was claimed as the inventor of the panpipe. Hyacinthus was
a youth loved and accidentally killed by Apollo, who caused the hyacinth to spring up from his blood as an
everlasting memorial.

Notes for the set *Trois chansons de Bilitis*

SOURCES
A: songs 1 and 2, "La flûte de Pan" and "La chevelure," at Paris, Bibliothèque nationale, manuscrit 1007.
Not dated. The autograph of song 3, "Le tombeau des Naïades," is in an inaccessible private collection. It is
dated 23 Aug. 1898 and dedicated to Madame Lucien Fontaine [according to M. Cobb, 1982].

A (supp.): Paris, Bibliothèque nationale, Manuscript 20636. An earlier draft of song 1, dated 22 June 1897.
A (supp.) contains fewer details of articulation, tempo, and expression and contains a piano part
incomplete in places.

E: Paris: Fromont, 1899. Contains no dedications, as followed here.
    Song 2 first appeared with incidental differences from source E in the revue *L'Image*, n. 11, Oct. 1897,
p. 339. It contains a dedication to Madame Alice Peter.

General Note for the set
    Certain dynamic and expressive indications occur in E that are not found in A or A (supp.). These
indications probably were added into the publisher's proofs by Debussy, which are untraced, and are included
here without further note.

Notes for "La flûte de Pan"

1. A (supp.) ties the l.h. diad ending m. 2 into m. 3. A and E are printed, considering the tenuto stress on the
downbeat added into source E.
2. A but not E: *retenu*.
3. A: no sharp to e^1, end of beat 3; E as printed.
4. A: *mf* m. 13; E *p* as printed.
5. A, m. 13 and 14; no natural to a, last chord r.h. E as printed.
6. A: no upper voice in l.h. (the chords on beats 2 and 3), which is inconsistent with m. 18. Debussy might
have intended the slight contrast, but the E reading is printed.

II. La chevelure
(The hair)

Il m'a dit: "Cette nuit, j'ai rêvé. J'avais
ta chevelure autour de mon cou. J'avais
tes cheveux comme un collier noir autour
de ma nuque et sur ma poitrine.

He told me: "Last night, I had a dream. I dreamed I had
your hair around my neck. I had
your hair like a black collar around
my neck and on my chest.

Je les caressais, et c'étaient les miens; et nous étions
liés pour toujours ainsi, par la même chevelure
la bouche sur la bouche, ainsi que deux lauriers n'ont
souvent qu'une racine.

"I caressed it, and it was mine; and we were
bound together always in that way, with the same hair,
mouth on mouth, like two laurels often have only
one root.

Et peu à peu, il m'a semblé, tant nos membres étaient
confondus, que je devenais toi-même ou que tu entrais
en moi comme mon songe."

"And little by little, it seemed, so much did our limbs
mingle that I became you, or that you entered
into me like a dream."

Quand il eut achevé, il mit doucement ses mains sur
mes épaules, et il me regarda d'un regard si tendre,
que je baissai les yeux avec un frisson.

When he had finished, he gently placed his hands on
my shoulders, and he looked at me with a look so tender,
that I lowered my eyes with a shudder.

Sources are indicated above for the set.

1. A, m. 1 beats 4-6 (and at lower octave l.h.):

E as printed, regarding the sequence of major 3rds and descending chromatic line apparently intended. This passage repeats in m. 20, where in source A a signal to repeat m. 1 appears for the piano part.
2. A: "Il me dit"; E and the Louÿs poem as printed.
3. A: no d-flat1, beats 4-6 m. 3-5, r.h.
4. A: r.h. chord that ends beat 3 repeats the chord that ends beats 1 and 2 (3rd triplet each time); E as printed.
5. E, m. 12 r.h. beat 2: f^3 not d^3; A as printed, analogous to the surrounding octaves.
6. A omits chord 3 of the r.h.
7. A: no b1, final chord r.h., and no c-sharp^2 m. 18, beat 3 r.h.
8. A: beat 2 r.h.: a-natural and not c-natural^1, and no sharp to f; E as printed.
9. A: m. 26 retains the natural to d^1 and d^2 on beat 5. E as printed with flat, needed for tonal stability at this conclusion.

III. Le tombeau des Naïades
(The tomb of the Naiads)

Le long du bois couvert de givre, je marchais;
mes cheveux devant ma bouche se fleurissaient
de petits glaçons, et mes sandales étaient lourdes
de neige fangeuse et tassée.

Through the woods covered with frost, I walked along;
my hair across my mouth bloomed
with little icicles, and my sandals were heavy
with mud and caked snow.

Il me dit: "Que cherches-tu!" "Je suis
la trace du satyre. Ses petits pas fourchus
alternent comme des trous dans un manteau blanc."
Il me dit: "Les satyres sont morts."

He spoke to me: "What are you looking for?" "I am
following the tracks of the satyr. His little, cloven footprints
are traced out like holes in a white cloak."
He said to me: "The satyrs are dead."

"Les satyres et les nymphes aussi. Depuis trente
ans il n'a pas fait un hiver aussi terrible. La trace
que tu vois est celle d'un bouc. Mais restons ici,
où est leur tombeau."

"The satyrs and the nymphs as well. For thirty
years there has not been so terrible a winter. The tracks
you see are those of a billy goat. But let us stay here,
where their tomb is."

Le tombeau des Naïades, continued

Et avec le fer de sa houe il cassa la glace de la source	*And with the blade of his hoe he broke the ice in the spring*
où jadis riaient les Naïades. Il prenait	*where the Naiads in years past used to laugh. He took up*
de grands morceaux froids, et les soulevant	*large, cold pieces, and holding them up*
vers le ciel pâle, il regardait au travers.	*to the pale sky, he peered through them.*

Notes on the text

      The naiads were nymphs, in ancient Greek mythology, who lived in and gave life to springs, fountains, and lakes. The satyr was a woodland deity having traits of a horse or goat and also of a man. He was associated with lust.

Sources for the set are indicated above. Lacking access to the autograph of "Le tombeau des Naïades," this edition refers entirely to source E.

Dans le jardin
(In the garden)

Je regardais dans le jardin,	*I peered into the garden,*
Furtif, au travers de la haie;	*Furtively, through the hedge;*
Je t'ai vue, enfant! et soudain,	*I saw you, a child! and suddenly,*
Mon cœur tressaillit: je t'aimais!	*My heart thrilled: I loved you!*
Je m'égratignais aux épines,	*I was scratched by the thorns,*
Mes doigts saignaient avec les mûres,	*My fingers bled along with the blackberries*
Et ma souffrance était divine:	*And my suffering was divine:*
Je voyais to front de gamine,	*I looked at your girlish brow,*
Tes cheveux d'or et ton front pur!	*Your golden hair and your pure face!*
Grandette et pour tant puérile,	*A grown girl and yet childlike,*
Coquette d'instinct seulement,	*Charming only by instinct,*
Les yeux bleus ombrés de longs cils,	*Your blue eyes shaded by long lashes*
Qui regardent tout gentiment,	*That look about so gently,*
Un corps un peu frêle et charmant,	*Your body a bit frail and charming,*
Une voix de mai, des gestes d'avril!	*A voice of May, with gestures of April!*
Je regardais dans le jardin,	*I peered into the garden,*
Furtif, au travers de la haie;	*Furtively, through the hedge;*
Je t'ai vue, enfant! et soudain,	*I saw you, a child! and suddenly,*
Mon cœur tressaillit: je t'aimais!	*My heart thrilled: I loved you!*

SOURCES
A: inaccessible private collection in the United States
E: Paris: Hamelle, 1905

1. E indicates *Retenu* at m. 26, *a tempo* at m. 30, and *poco rit.* at m. 33. Such a fluctuation seems inconsistent with the continuum of rhythm in the accompaniment, and the *poco rit.* appears redundant preceding the *Retenu* (m. 34). These tedious indications are deleted here.
2. E qualifies the *Retenu* at the conclusion perhaps excessively: *Plus retenu* at m. 69, *Pressez* at m. 73-75, and *Très retenu* at m. 76. The performer will be advised to regard the spirit of a subtle *ad libitum*.
3. The variant pitches in the voice, m. 72-73, appear in E. The lower ones are preferred.

Fêtes galantes, série II

I. Les ingénus
(The ingenuous ones)

Les hauts talons luttaient avec les longues jupes,	*High heels would clash with long skirts,*
En sorte que, selon le terrain et le vent,	*So that, according to the terrain or the wind,*
Parfois luisaient des bas de jambes, trop souvent	*Sometimes a lower leg shone out, too often*
Interceptés! —et nous aimions ce jeu de dupes.	*Intercepted! and how we did love this trickster's game.*
Parfois aussi le dard d'un insecte jaloux	*Sometimes too the sting of a jealous insect*
Inquiétait le col des belles sous les branches,	*Disturbed the neck of the beauties beneath the branches,*
Et c'étaient des éclairs soudains de nuques blanches	*And there were sudden flashes of white napes*
Et ce régal comblait nos jeunes yeux de fous.	*And this treat satisfied our young foolish eyes.*
Le soir tombait, un soir équivoque d'automne:	*The evening would fall, an ambiguous autumn evening:*
Les belles, se pendant rêveuses à nos bras,	*The beauties, leaning dreamily on our arms,*
Dirent alors des mots si spécieux, tout bas,	*Would then say words so insincere, beneath their voice,*
Que notre âme depuis ce temps tremble et s'étonne.	*That our souls ever since have trembled in wonder.*

Notes for *Fêtes galantes, series II*

SOURCES
A1: Paris, Bibliothèque nationale, Manuscrit 17734. A1 differs in numerous details from A2 and is considered supplemental.
A2: Paris, B.n., Ms. 996. The fair copy used by Durand in engraving the edition.
E: Paris: Durand, 1904.
      One also might note a 1906 re-issue that contains both French and English texts. It transposes songs 1 and 2 up a minor third and song 3 up a major third.

General note: The dedication to Emma Bardac appears in Source A1 and is repeated in a letter to the publisher: "I ask you please not to forget the dedication: 'to thank the month of June 1904,' followed by the letters 'A.1.p.M.' It's a little mysterious, but something must be done for the legend."
      The letters stand for "A la petite Mienne," "for my dear little one." Emma Bardac would become Debussy's beloved second wife and kindred spirit. However, both the composer and Emma were still married to their first spouses at the time of publication, and protocol must have suggested that the dedication be omitted from the editon. It is contained here, since Debussy clearly intended it.

Notes for "Les ingénus"

1. Debussy's indications of dynamics are retained except as noted. Throughout Fêtes galantes II, however, they are more symbolic than practicable. The performers might follow their general sense while raising the dynamic level slightly.
2. A2: no change of dynamic level m. 20 and 26; E as printed.
3. E sustains the f^2 in the voice, m. 34, through m. 35; A1 and A2 as printed, which is consistent with the subtle quality of the vocal line.

II. Le faune
(The faun)

Un vieux faune de terre cuite	*An old terra-cotta faun*
Rit au centre des boulingrins,	*Laughs from the center of the bowling green,*
Présageant sans doute une suite	*Predicting, no doubt, a bad outcome*
Mauvaise à ces instants sereins	*To these serene moments*
Qui m'ont conduit et t'ont conduite,	*That have led me and you,*
—Mélancoliques pèlerins,—	*—Melancholy pilgrims,—*
Jusqu'à cette heure dont la fuite	*To this very hour, the quick passage of which*
Tournoie au son des tambourins.	*Swirls to the sound of the tambourines.*

Le faune, continued

Note on the text: In Greek myth, the faun differed little from the satyr, having a goat's body with the head and hands of a man.

Sources are indicated above for the set.

1. A1 and A2: ⎯⎯⎯⎯ at m. 2, seemingly redundant and omitted from E (printed).
2. A1 and A2: no *avec une expression sourde;* E as printed.
3. E (printed): no low bass slur, as contrasted with previous measures. A2 appears not to continue the slurs, even though it indicates only a shorthand measure-repeat for the bass of m. 17.
4. A2 and E again omit the bass slur m. 28-33, suggesting Debussy's conception of separated articulation. A2 does not contain *Un peu animé* at m. 24 or *a Tempo* m. 28; these were probably added by Debussy to the publisher's proofs.
5. E: *pp* preceding and following the ⎯⎯⎯⎯ ; A2 as printed, without the impractical second *pp.*

III. Colloque sentimental
(Sentimental Conversation)

Dans le vieux parc solitaire et glacé,   *In the old park, lonely and frozen,*
Deux formes ont tout à l'heure passé.   *Two forms have just now passed by.*

Leurs yeux sont morts et leurs lèvres sont molles,   *Their eyes are dead and their lips are slack,*
Et l'on entend à peine leurs paroles.   *And one barely hears their words.*

Dans le vieux parc solitaire et glacé,   *In the old park, lonely and frozen,*
Deux spectres ont évoqué le passé.   *Two specters have evoked the past.*

—Te souvient-il de notre extase ancienne?   *—Do you still remember our former ecstasy?*
—Pourquoi voulez-vous donc qu'il m'en souvienne?   *—Why do you want me to remember it?*

—Ton cœur bat-il toujours à mon seul nom?   *—Does your heart still beat merely at my name?*
Toujours vois-tu mon âme en rêve? Non.   *Do you still see my soul in your dreams? No.*

—Ah! Les beaux jours de bonheur indicible   *—Ah! Those beautiful days of inexpressible happiness*
Où nous joignions nos bouches! —C'est possible.   *When we joined our lips together! It is possible.*

—Qu'il était bleu, le ciel, et grand l'espoir!   *—How blue was the sky, and how great our hope!*
—L'espoir a fui, vaincu, vers le ciel noir.   *—Hope has fled, vanquished, into the black sky.*

Tels ils marchaient dans les avoines folles,   *Thus they walked through the wild oats,*
Et la nuit seule entendit leurs paroles.   *And only the night heard their words.*

Sources are indicated above for the set.

1. E: ⎯⎯⎯⎯ up to end of measure; A2 as printed, with ⎯⎯⎯⎯
2. E ties the final two notes, b-flat, in the r.h.; A2 as printed, considering the separation implied by the tenuto mark.
3. A2: no *Plus lent*; E as printed.

Trois chansons de France
(Three Songs of France)

I. Rondel ("Le temps")
(Rondel: The weather has shed its cloak)

Le temps a laissié son manteau   *The weather has shed its cloak*
De vent, de froidure et de pluye,   *Of wind, cold, and rain,*
Et s'est vestu de broderye,   *And has dressed in embroidery,*
De soleil raiant, cler et beau.   *Which is the radiant sun, clear and fine.*

Rondel ("Le temps), continued

Il n'y a beste ne oiseau	*There is neither beast nor bird*
Qui en son jargon ne chante ou crye:	*Who in his language does not sing or cry:*
Le temps a laissié son manteau.	*The weather has shed its cloak.*
Rivière, fontaine et ruisseau	*River, fountain, and brook*
Portent, en livrée jolye,	*All wear, in joyful livery,*
Goutes d'argent d'orfaverie.	*Drops of silver and gold.*
Chascun s'abille de nouveau,	*Each is adorned anew,*
Le temps a laissié son manteau.	*The weather has shed its cloak.*

Notes for the set *Trois chansons de France*

SOURCES
A: Paris, Bibliothèque nationale, Ms. 981 [1904]
E: Paris: Durand, 1904. The dedication is to Madame S. Bardac, the future Madame Deussy. See the note above concerning the dedication Debussy intended for *Fêtes galantes*, series II.

Song 2, "La grotte," was republished without revision in 1910, as song 1 of the set *Le promenoir des deux amants.*

Notes for "Rondel: Le temps a laissié"

1. A: m. 18 and 19, no natural to a^1, r.h.; E as printed.
2. A: no crescendo m. 29
3. A and E: *f*; the editorial change to *mf* seems logical preceding the crescendo to *f*.

II. La grotte
(The grotto)

Auprès de cette grotte sombre	*Near this dark grotto*
Où l'on respire un air si doux,	*Where one breathes an air so sweet,*
L'onde lutte avec les cailloux,	*The tide struggles against the pebbles,*
Et la lumière avecque l'ombre.	*And light against shadow.*
Ces flots, lassés de l'exercice	*These waves, weary from the effort*
Qu'ils ont fait dessus ce gravier,	*That they exerted moving across the gravel,*
Se reposent dans ce vivier	*Rest in the pond*
Où mourût autrefois Narcisse…	*Where in bygone days Narcissus died…*
L'ombre de cette fleur vermeille	*The shadow of this vermillion flower*
Et celle de ces joncs pendants	*And that of the bending rushes*
Paraissent estre là dedans	*Appear to be there amid*
Les songes de l'eau qui sommeille.	*The dreams of the sleeping water.*

Note on the text
      Narcissus in Greek mythology was caused by the gods to pine his life away for love of his own reflection, and is memorialized in the narcissus flower.

Editorial note for "La grotte"
      The song was republished without revision by Durand in 1910, as song 1 of the set *Le promenoir des deux amants*, under the title *Auprès de cette grotte sombre.*

Sources are indicated above for the set.

III. Rondel ("Pour ce que Plaisance")
(Rondel: Because pleasure is dead)

Pour ce que Plaisance est morte	*Because Pleasure is dead*
Ce may, suis vestu de noir;	*This May, I am dressed in black;*
C'est grand pitié de véoir	*It is a great pity to see*
Mon cœur qui s'en desconforte.	*My heart, which is thus discomforted.*
Je m'abille de la sorte	*I dress in a manner*
Que doy, pour faire devoir;	*That I must, out of duty;*
Pour ce que Plaisance est morte,	*Because Pleasure is dead*
Ce may, suis vestu de noir.	*This May, I am dressed in black.*
Le temps ces nouvelles porte	*The weather brings this news*
Qui ne veut déduit avoir;	*That brooks no diversion;*
Mais par force du plouvoir	*But because of it a strong rain*
Fait des champs clore la porte,	*Makes the fields close their doors,*
Pour ce que Plaisance est morte.	*Because Pleasure is dead.*

Sources are indicated above for the set.

1. E: no diad a-flat/c^1 in r.h. That reading in source A is printed, by analogy with its structural and harmonic parallel in m. 4.

Le promenoir des deux amants
(The Promenade of the Two Lovers)

Number 1 of this set, "La grotte" ("Auprès de cette grotte"), was first published in 1904 as number 2 in the set *Trois chansons de France,* which see previously.

II. Crois mon conseil, chère Clième
(Take my advice, dear Climene)

Crois mon conseil, chère Climène;	*Take my advice, dear Climene;*
Pour laisser arriver le soir,	*To await the fall of evening,*
Je te prie, allons nous asseoir	*I beg of you, let us sit*
Sur le bord de cette fontaine.	*At the edge of this fountain.*
N'oüis-tu pas soupirer Zéphire,	*Do you not hear Zephyr sighing,*
De merveille et d'amour atteint,	*Struck by wonder and love,*
Voyant des roses sur ton teint,	*Upon seeing the roses in your complexion,*
Qui ne sont pas de son empire?	*Which are not in his power?*
Sa bouche d'odeur toute pleine,	*His mouth full of perfume,*
A soufflé sur notre chemin,	*Has blown upon our path,*
Mêlant un esprit de jasmin	*Mixing a breath of jasmine*
A l'ambre de ta douce haleine.	*With the amber of your sweet breath.*

Notes for the set *Le promenoir des deux amants*

SOURCES
A: Paris, Bibliothèque nationale, Manuscrit 1027 [1910, songs 2 and 3].

> Contains the dedication "à Emma Claude Debussy…p.m. son mari C.D." ["for Emma Claude Debussy…my dear one (petite mienne) her husband Claude Debussy"].

Crois mon conseil chère Climène, continued

Notes for "Crois mon conseil, chère Climène"

1. A: no *decrescendo* m. 9, no *Cédez un peu* m. 10, and no *au Mouvt* m. 12. E as printed, probably following Debussy's emendations to the publisher's proofs preceding the publication.
2. A but not E: the sign // following *Cédez,* indicating the end of slowing the tempo.
3. A and E r.h. upper line give ♪♩♪ , although the vertical alignment requires the rhythm as printed.

III. Je tremble en voyant ton visage
(I tremble when I see your face)

Je tremble en voyant ton visage	*I tremble when I see your face*
Flotter avecque mes désirs,	*Floating with my desires,*
Tant j'ai de peur que mes soupirs	*So much do I fear that my sighs*
Ne lui fassent faire naufrage.	*Might shipwreck it.*
De crainte de cette aventure	*For fear of this adventure*
Ne commets pas si librement	*Do not commit so freely*
A cet infidèle élément	*To this faithless element*
Tous les trésors de la Nature.	*All the treasures of Nature.*
Veux-tu, par un doux privilège,	*Do you wish, by some sweet privilege,*
Me mettre au-dessus des humains?	*To place me above humans?*
Fais-moi boire au creux de tes mains,	*Make me drink from the cup of your hands,*
Si l'eau n'en dissout point la neige.	*If water does not melt their snow.*

Sources are indicated above for the set.

1. A: "Tant j'ai peur" instead of the reading in E (printed), "Tant j'ai de peur." In source A the vocal rhythm of beat 3 is of 2 duplets, on the pitches f^1 and b-flat^1.
2. E: no double dot in r.h. and no 32nd note flag; A as printed.
3. A: no decrescendo in voice, m. 19; E with decrescendo as printed.

Trois ballades de François Villon
(Three Ballads by François Villon)

I. Ballade [Ballade de Villon à s'amye]
(Villon's Ballad to his Lady)

Faulse beauté, qui tant me couste cher,	*False beauty, who costs me so dearly,*
Rude en effect, hypocrite doulceur,	*In truth cruel, hypocritical sweetness,*
Amour dure, plus que fer, à mascher;	*Hard love, harder than iron to chew;*
Nommer te puis de ma deffaçon sœur.	*I could even call you the sister of my ruin.*
Charme felon, la mort d'ung povre cueur,	*Felonious charm, the death of a poor heart,*
Orgueil mussé, qui gens met au mourir,	*Concealed pride that puts men to death,*
Yeulx sans pitié! ne veult droict de rigueur,	*Pitiless eyes! Will not hard justice,*
Sans empirer, ung povre secourir?	*Without worsening his lot, help a poor man?*
Mieulx m'eust valu avoir esté crier	*Better for me to have gone*
Ailleurs secours, c'eust esté mon bonheur:	*Elsewhere for help, that would have been happiness:*
Rien ne m'eust sceu de ce fait arracher;	*Nothing would have been able to tear me from this reality;*
Trotter m'en fault en fuyte à deshonneur.	*Flee I must, now, in disgrace.*
Haro, haro, le grand et le mineur!	*Shame, shame, great and small!*
Et qu'est cecy? mourray sans coup ferir,	*And what is this? I shall die without striking a blow,*
Ou pitié peult, selon ceste teneur,	*Or pity can, according to his refrain,*
Sans empirer, ung povre secourir.	*Without worsening his lot, help a poor man.*

Ballade de Villon à s'amye, continued

Ung temps viendra, qui fera desseicher,	*A time shall come that will wither away,*
Jaulnir, flestrir, vostre espanie fleur:	*Fade, wilt away your opened flower:*
J'en risse lors, se tant peusse marcher,	*I shall laugh then, if I can still walk,*
Mais las! nenny: Ce seroye donc foleur,	*But alas! nay: that would be folly,*
Vieil je seray; vous, laide et sans couleur.	*Old I shall be; and you ugly and colorless.*
Or, beuvez fort, tant que ru peult courir.	*So drink hardy now, as long as the brook can flow.*
Ne donnez pas à tous ceste douleur,	*Do not contribute to all this same misery,*
Sans empirer ung povre secourir.	*Without worsening his lot, help a poor man.*
Prince amoureux, des amans le greigneur,	*Amorous Prince, lord of lovers,*
Vostre mal gré ne vouldroye encourir;	*Your ill will I would not incur;*
Mais tout franc cueur doit, par Nostre Seigneur,	*But every good heart must, by Our Lord,*
Sans empirer, ung povre secourir.	*Without worsening his lot, help a poor man.*

Note on the text

Villon's ballad salutes Charles d'Orléans, poet prince, and contains the rhetoric typical of late-medieval courtly poetry. It exhibits, furthermore, the realism and irony of the Renaissance era to come.

Notes for the set *Trois ballades de François Villon*

SOURCES

A: Paris, Bibilothèque nationale, manuscrit 974. Dated "Mai 1910."
A (supp): Paris, Bibliothèque nationale, manuscrit 975. The later, orchestral version of 1911.
E1: Paris: Durand, 1910
E2: Paris: Durand, 1911. The published edition with orchestral accompaniment by the composer, containing a few autograph corrections by Debussy. Carlton Lake Collection, Harry Ransom Humanities Research Center, University of Texas at Austin.

General note on the sources: Source A differs from E1 by containing fewer indications of dynamics, tempo, articulation, and expression. Those in E1 are printed here except as noted, since emendations to A probably occurred in the publisher's proofs. E1 is considered the basic source, although the variants in A and E2 are cited in the notes below.

Notes for "Ballade de Villon à s'amye"

1. A: slur over l.h. for entire m. 3
2. A inadvertently omits beats 3 and 4 in the low bass.
3. A: no slur in l.h. at m. 19, 22, 23, and beats 1-2 of m. 24.
4. A: no sharp to d^2 in voice.
5. A: neither slurs nor staccato dots as E (printed) for the voice, m. 32-34, 41, and 48.
6. A: no slur in l.h. beats 1 and 3, in m. 36, 39-40, 47-48.
7. E ends *serrez* by // at end of m. 37 and places *Mouvt,* as printed, m. 39. A omits all these indications. The *retenu* as printed is implied, m. 38.

II. Ballade

que Villon feit à la requeste de sa mère pour prier Nostre-Dame
(Ballad that Villon wrote at the request of his mother to pray to Our Lady)

Dame du ciel, régente terrienne,	*Lady of heaven, earthly regent,*
Emperière des infernaulx palux,	*Empress of the infernal depths,*
Recevez-moy vostre humble chrestienne,	*Receive me, your humble Christian,*
Que comprinse soye entre vos esleuz,	*That I may be counted among your elect,*
Ce non obstant qu'oncques riens ne valuz.	*Even though I never had anything of value.*
Les biens de vous, ma dame et ma maistresse,	*Your goodnesss, my lady and my mistress,*
Sont trop plus grans que ne suys pecheresse,	*Is even greater than my sinfulness,*
Sans lesquelz bien ame ne peult merir	*Without that goodness no soul can merit*
N'avoir les cieulx, je n'en suis menteresse.	*Nor gain heaven, I am truthful now.*
En ceste foy je vueil vivre et mourir.	*In this faith I would live and die.*

Ballade que Villon feit à la requeste de sa mére pour prier Nostre-Dame, continued

A vostre Filz dictes que je suys sienne;	*To your Son say that I am his own;*
De luy soyent mes pechez aboluz:	*By him may my sins be absolved:*
Pardonnez-moy comme l'Egyptienne,	*Forgive me as he forgave the Egyptian woman,*
Ou comme il feit au clerc Théophilus,	*Or as he did the clerk Theophilus,*
Lequel par vous fut quitte et aboluz,	*Who was acquitted and absolved by you,*
Combien qu'il eust au diable faict promesse.	*Although he had made a pact with the devil.*
Preservez-moy que je n'accomplisse ce!	*Preserve me from doing the same!*
Vierge portant sans rompure encourir	*Virgin bearing without incurring blemish*
Le sacrement qu'on celebre à la messe.	*The sacrament that we celebrate at mass.*
En ceste foy je vueil vivre et mourir.	*In this faith I would live and die.*
Femme je suis povrette et ancienne,	*A woman I am, poor and old,*
Qui riens ne sçay; oncques lettre ne leuz;	*Who knows nothing, and cannot read;*
Au moustier voy dont suis paroissienne,	*At the monastery where I am a parishioner,*
Paradis painct où sont harpes et luz,	*Paradise is painted there, with harps and lutes,*
Et ung enfer où damnez sont boulluz:	*And a hell where the damned are boiled:*
L'ung me faict paour, l'aultre joye et liesse.	*The one makes me fearful, the other joyful and glad.*
La joye avoir fais-moy, haulte Déesse,	*Make me have that joy, high Goddess,*
A qui pecheurs doibvent tous recourir,	*You to whom all sinners must return.*
Comblez de foy, sans faincte ne paresse.	*Filled with faith, without hypocrisy or weakness of spirit.*
En ceste foy je vueil vivre et mourir.	*In this faith I would live and die.*

Note on the text

Villon, an outcast and criminal, was awaiting a death sentence when he wrote this poem. Here he adopts the piety of his mother, whether as a poetic device or, imitating her, as an expression of his own contrition.

Sources are indicated above for the set.

1. A: no slur in vocal line m. 8
2. E2 adds by autograph *poco* preceding the crescendo.
3. E1: no stem down to *a*, m. 20 l.h. beat 4. E2 sustains the *a* in viola II.
4. E1 and E2: no f[1] in r.h., last half of beat 4. Source A allows the r.h. to continue doubling the voice at this passage and includes the f[1].
5. A: no b-natural, m. 26 l.h. second half of beat 3.
6. A: no slurs m. 30
7. A: no slurs in voice, m. 37-46, or in r.h. at m. 40.
8. A: f[1] ♩ , l.h. m. 41 beat 2; E1 and E2 as printed, with moving figure. A also contains diad a-flat[1]/b-flat[1] half note (♩) a-flat[1]/b-flat[1] half note (♩), beats 1-2, and the same an octave lower, beats 3-4.
9. E1: b-flat ♩ in l.h., beats 3-4 as well as 1-2; A and E2 (by autograph correction to French horn III) as printed, without sustaining b-flat at beats 3-4, measures 41 and 42.

III. Ballade des femmes de Paris
(Ballad of the Women of Paris)

Quoy qu'on tient belles langagières	*Although one may consider as fine talkers*
Florentines, Veniciennes,	*Florentine or Venetian women,*
Assez pour estre messaigières,	*Good enough to be messengers,*
Et mesmement les anciennes;	*And even the old ones;*
Mais, soient Lombardes, Romaines,	*But, be it the Lombards, Romans,*
Genevoises, à mes périls,	*Women of Genoa, I dare say,*
Piemontoises, Savoysiennes,	*The women of the Piedmont or Savoy,*
Il n'est bon bec que de Paris.	*There is no gift of gab as in Paris.*

Ballade des femmes de Paris, continued

De beau parler tiennent chayères,	*In fine speech they hold a chair,*
Ce dit-on Napolitaines,	*They say of the Neapolitans,*
Et que sont bonnes cacquetières	*And that they are the good chatterers,*
Allemandes et Bruciennes;	*The Germans and Prussians;*
Soient Grecques, Egyptiennes,	*Be they Greeks, Egyptians,*
De Hongrie ou d'aultre païs,	*From Hungary or other lands,*
Espaignolles ou Castellannes,	*Spanish or Castilian,*
Il n'est bon bec que de Paris.	*There is no gift of gab as in Paris.*
Brettes, Suysses, n'y sçavent guères,	*The women of Brittany or the Swiss, scarcely do they know,*
Ne Gasconnes et Tholouzaines;	*Nor do the Gascons or the women of Toulouse;*
Du Petit-Pont deux harangères	*On the Petit Pont two fishwives*
Les concluront, et les Lorraines,	*Would do them in, and the women from Lorraine,*
Anglesches ou Callaisiennes,	*The English or those from Calais,*
(Ay-je beaucoup de lieux compris?)	*(Have I included enough places?)*
Picardes, de Valenciennes…	*From Picardy or Valenciennes…*
Il n'est bon bec que de Paris.	*There is no gift of gab as in Paris.*
Prince, aux dames parisiennes,	*Prince, to the women of Paris*
De bien parler donnez le prix;	*Give the prize for good and strong talk;*
Quoy qu'on die d'Italiennes,	*Whatever one may say of the Italians,*
Il n'est bon bec que de Paris.	*There is no gift of gab as in Paris.*

Sources are indicated above for the set.

General note: The voice part of source A contains sparse articulation marks. These no doubt were added by Debussy to the publisher's proofs. Singers are advised to observe the fine distinctions of articulation and emphasis, here as throughout the songs.

1. A: no sharp to *a*, l.h.
2. E2 by autograph correction, but not A or E1: *Meno mosso* m. 35 and *molto* following *rubato* m. 43.
3. A: no expressive indication; E1 as printed; E2: the indication *Rubato* is printed in the score.
4. E2 *pp* at m. 109 printed, and *p* ⎯⎯⎯⎯⎯ at m. 108. A and E1 as printed, appropriate for piano-vocal scoring.
5. A: *Un peu retenu* at m. 117, but no *en animant* previously at m. 109. E1: *En animant* m. 109, *au Mouvement* at m. 117, and no further tempo indications. E2: *En animant* at m. 109, no indication *au Mouvement* m. 117, by autograph emendation *Cédez* m. 119-120, and *Mouvt.* [*a tempo*] m. 121. Furthermore, Debussy added by autograph correction to E2 an accompaniment of chromatic filler in the brass, m. 119, to join the brass accompaniment printed for m. 120. The orchestral version must have suggested a more dramatic ending than appropriate in A and E1; therefore, the ending of E1 is retained, adding *cédez-mouvement* only for m. 120-21.

Trois poèmes de Stéphane Mallarmé
(Three poems of Stéphane Mallarmé)

I. Soupir
(Sigh)

Mon âme vers ton front où rêve, ô calme sœur,	*My soul rises up toward your brow where dreams, o calm sister,*
Un automne jonché de taches de rousseur	*An autumn strewn with freckles*
Et vers le ciel errant de ton œil angélique	*And toward the shifting heaven of your angelic eyes*
Monte, comme dans un jardin mélancolique,	*As, in a melancholy garden,*
Fidèle, un blanc jet d'eau soupire vers l'Azur!	*Faithfully, a white fountain sighs for the azure sky!*
Vers l'Azur attendri d'Octobre pâle et pur	*Toward the tender azure of a pale and pure October*
Qui mire aux grands bassins sa langueur infinie	*That mirrors in the great basins its infinite languor*
Et laisse, sur l'eau morte où la fauve agonie	*And lets, on the dead water where the fawn-colored death agony*
Des feuilles erre au vent et creuse un froid sillon,	*Of the leaves roams in the wind and plows a cold furrow,*
Se traîner le soleil jaune d'un long rayon.	*The sun trail out in a long ray.*

Notes for *Trois poèmes de Stéphane Mallarmé*

SOURCES
A: Paris, Bibliothèque nationale, manuscrit 1028. Dated "1913 (Été)."
E: Paris: Durand, 1913. The complete dedication reads: "à la mémoire de Stéphane Mallarmé et en très respectueux hommage à Madame E. Bonniot (née G. Mallarmé)" ["to the memory of Stéphane Mallarmé and in respectful homage to Madame E. Bonniot (née G. Mallarmé)"]. Geneviève Mallarmé was the poet's daughter.

   Note that many indications of dynamics, tempo and expression appear in E but not A, added doubtless at the proof stage. These are printed without further comment.

Notes for "Soupir"

1. Measures 1-3, E as printed; A (voice tacet):

2. A: m.9, the reminder flat to e^3 and d^3, r.h., is found in A and E, as are the naturals ti e^1 and d^1, l.h. M. 10, A beats 1 and 2 gives flats to e^1 and e^3, and natural to d^1 in l.h. but not to d^3 r.h. E as printed, keeping m.9 and 10 parallel.

II. Placet futile
(Futile petition)

Princesse! à jalouser le destin d'une Hébé	*Princess! jealous of the fate of a Hebe*
Qui poind sur cette tasse au baiser de vos lèvres,	*Who springs from this cup at the kiss of your lips,*
J'use mes feux mais n'ai rang discret que d'abbé	*I waste my ardor but have only the modest rank of an abbot*
Et ne figurerai même nu sur le Sèvres.	*And will never appear, even nude, on a Sèvres cup.*
Comme je ne suis pas ton bichon embarbé,	*As I am not your bearded lapdog,*
Ni la pastille, ni du rouge, ni jeux mièvres	*Nor pastille, nor rouge, nor dainty games*
Et que sur moi je sais ton regard clos tombé,	*And as I know your closed eyes fall on me thus,*
Blonde dont les coiffeurs divins sont des orfèvres!	*Blond whose heavenly coiffeurs are goldsmiths!*
Nommez-nous… toi de qui tant de ris framboisés	*Choose us… you from whom so many raspberry smiles*
Se joignent en troupeau d'agneaux apprivoisés	*Join in a troup of tamed lambs*
Chez tous broutant les vœux et bêlant aux délires,	*Which for all men graze on desire and bleat in ecstasy,*
Nommez-nous… pour qu'Amour ailé d'un éventail	*Choose us…so that Amor with wings like a fan*
M'y peigne flûte aux doigts endormant ce bercail,	*Might comb me, flute in hand and putting this sheepfold to sleep,*
Princesse, nommez-nous berger de vous sourires.	*Princess, choose us as the shepherd of your smiles.*

Placet futile, continued

Sources are indicated above for the set.

1. A but not E: slur over entire measure of r.h.

III. Éventail
(Fan)

O rêveuse, pour que je plonge	*O dreamer, so that I might plunge*
Au pur délice sans chemin,	*Into pure pathless delight,*
Sache, par un subtil mensonge,	*Take care, by some subtle deceit,*
Garder mon aile dans ta main.	*To keep my wing in your hand.*
Une fraîcheur de crépuscule	*A freshness of twilight*
Te vient à chaque battement	*Comes to you at each flutter*
Dont le coup prisonnier recule	*By which the imprisoned stroke drives away*
L'horizon délicatement.	*The horizon, delicately.*
Vertige! voici que frissone	*Vertigo! Here space*
L'espace comme un grand baiser	*Shivers like a great kiss*
Qui, fou de naître pour personne,	*That, enraged at being born for no one,*
Ne peut jaillir ni s'apaiser.	*Can neither come forth nor be stilled.*
Sens-tu le paradis farouche	*Do you sense the wild paradise*
Ainsi qu'un rire enseveli	*Like a fierce but shy laugh*
Se couler du coin de ta bouche	*Flowing from the corner of your mouth*
Au fond de l'unanime pli!	*Into the depths of the concealed folds!*
Le sceptre des rivages roses	*The sceptre of rose shores*
Stagnants sur les soirs d'or, ce l'est,	*Stagnant beneath golden evenings, this it is,*
Ce blanc vol fermé que tu poses	*This closed white flight that you rest*
Contre le feu d'un bracelet.	*Against the fire of a bracelet.*

Note on the text
      The person addressing the young lady relates to and even covets the favored position of her fan. All 3 of these Mallarmé poems allude to the poet's daughter.

Sources are indicated above for the set.

1. A, m. 34-35, gives a fourth figure in r.h. of each measure (♫♫♫),which repeats the third figure of each measure. E as printed.
2. A gives the following figure in the l.h., m. 46:

Noël des enfants qui n'ont plus de maisons
(Christmas carol for homeless children)

Nous n'avons plus de maisons!	*We have no homes!*
Les ennemis ont tout pris,	*The enemy has taken all,*
tout pris, tout pris,	*has taken all, all,*
jusqu'à notre petit lit!	*down to our little beds!*
Ils ont brûlé l'école et notre maître aussi.	*They have burned the school and our schoolmaster too.*
Ils ont brûlé l'église et monsieur Jésus-Christ	*The have burned the church and Mr. Jesus Christ*
Et le vieux pauvre qui n'a pas pu s'en aller!	*And the poor old man who couldn't get away!*
Nous n'avons plus de maisons.	*We have no homes.*
Les ennemis ont tout pris,	*The enemy has taken all,*
tout pris, tout pris,	*has taken all, all,*
jusqu'à notre petit lit!	*down to our little beds!*
Bien sûr! papa est à la guerre,	*Of course! papa is away at war,*
Pauvre maman est morte!	*Poor mama is dead!*
Avant d'avoir vu tout ça.	*Before seeing all of that.*

Noël des enfants qui n'ont plus de maisons, continued

Qu'est-ce que l'on va faire?	*What shall we do?*
Noël! petit Noël! n'allez pas chez eux,	*Christmas! little Christmas! Don't go to them,*
n'allez plus jamais chez eux,	* never go again to them.*
Punissez-les!	*Punish them!*
Vengez les enfants de France!	*Avenge the children of France!*
Les petits Belges, les petits Serbes,	*The little Belgians, the little Serbs,*
et les petits Polonais aussi!	* and the little Poles too!*
Si nous en oublions, pardonnez-nous.	*If we forget any, forgive us.*
Noël! Noël! surtout, pas de joujoux,	*Christmas! Christmas! above all no toys,*
Tâchez de nous redonner le pain quotidien.	*Just try to give us our daily bread.*
Nous n'avons plus de maisons!	*We have no homes!*
Les ennemis ont tout pris,	*The enemy has taken all,*
tout pris, tout pris,	* has taken all, all,*
jusqu'à notre petit lit!	* down to our little beds!*
Ils ont brûlé l'école et notre maître aussi.	*They have burned the school and our schoolmaster too.*
Ils ont brûlé l'église et monsieur Jésus Christ	*They have burned the church and Mr. Jesus Christ*
Et le vieux pauvre qui n'a pas pu s'en aller!	*And the poor old man who couldn't get away!*
Noël! écoutez-nous, nous n'avons plus de petits sabots:	*Christmas! Hear us, we have no little shoes:*
Mais donnez la victoire aux enfants de France!	*But give the victory to the children of France!*

SOURCES
A: Paris, Bibliothèque nationale, manuscrit 1023
E: Paris: Durand, 1916

General note: Debussy wrote the French text for this work, a Christmas carol for children made homeless by World War I. Source E contained an English translation by Mme. Swayne St.-René Taillandier; such a translation was a unique case for the first edition of Debussy songs. The composer also arranged the "Noël" for children's choir and piano.

1. E: m. 12-13 and 69-70, gives diads stemmed together in l.h., whereas A (as printed) distinguishes 2 lines in l.h. by giving differing stem directions.
2. A, m. 80, l.h. beat 3, and m. 82, r.h. beat 2, continues the repeating triplet figure. E as printed, perhaps to help avoid fatiguing the pianist.

Songs of Claude Debussy

Volume II: Medium Voice

Deux romances

Published 1891

I. Romance: L'âme évaporée

Paul Bourget

II. Les cloches [1]

Paul Bourget

Les angélus

1891

Grégoire Le Roy

Trois mélodies de Paul Verlaine
1891

I. La mer est plus belle

à Ernest Chausson

Paul Verlaine

La mer est plus bel - le Que les ca - thé -

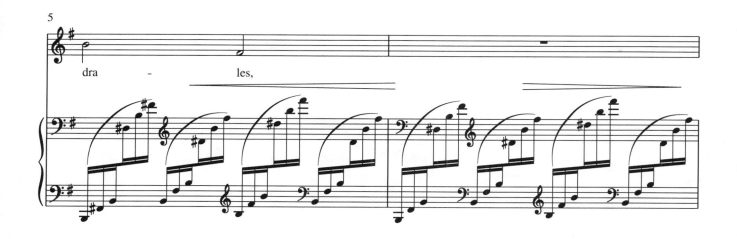

dra - les,

II. Le son du cor

1891

à Robert Godet

Paul Verlaine

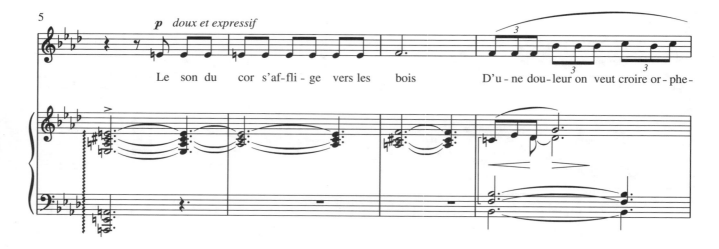

Le son du cor s'af-fli-ge vers les bois D'u-ne dou-leur on veut croire or-phe-

li - ne Qui vient mou-rir au bas de la col-li-ne Par-mi la

bise er - rant en courts a - bois.

Un peu animé

L'â - me du loup pleu - re dans cet - te

voix Qui monte a - vec le so - leil qui dé - cli - ne

D'une a - go - nie on veut croi - re ca - li - ne Et qui ra - vit et qui navre à la

fois.

1er Mouvement

Pour fai - re mieux cet - te plainte as - sou -

III. L'échelonnement des haies

1891

à Robert Godet

Paul Verlaine

Assez vif et gaiement

L'é - che - lon - ne - ment des haies Mou - tonne à l'in - fi - ni, mer

Fêtes galantes, série I

1891 - 1892

I. En sourdine[1]

1892
à Madame Robert Godet

Paul Verlaine

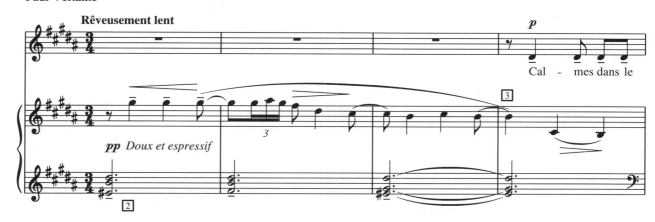

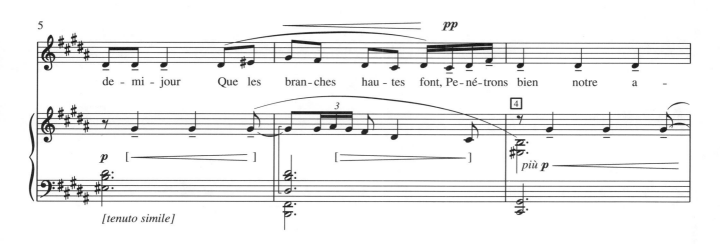

52

mi Chasse à ja - mais tout des - sein.

molto dim.

pp

Intimement doux [Plus lent]

Lais - sons - nous per - su - a - der Au

Animé
poco cresc.

souf - fle ber - ceur et doux Qui vient à tes pieds ri -

poco cresc.

[rit.]

Un peu plus lent [1er Mouvt.]

der Les on - des de ga - zon roux.

mf dim. [e rit.]

p

II. Fantoches

1891

à Madame Lucien Fontaine

Paul Verlaine

Sca - ra - mouche et Pul - ci - nel - la Qu'un mau - vais des -

sein ras - sem - bla Ges - ti - cu - lent, noirs sous la lu - ne, la la la la la

56

par - mi l'her - be bru - ne.

Lors sa fil - le, pi - quant mi -

nois, Sous la __ char - mil - le, en __ ta - pi -

nois, Se glis - se de - mi nu - e __ la la la la la

la la la la la la la _____ en
quê - - te De ___ son ___ beau ___ pi -
rate es - pa - gnol, Dont un a - mou -
reux ros - si - gnol _____ Cla - me la dé - tresse à tue-

III. Clair de lune

1891

à Madame Arthur Fontaine

Paul Verlaine

Jou - ant du luth et dan - sant et qua - si

Tris - tes sous leurs dé - gui - se - ments fan - tas - ques.

Tout en chant - tant sur le mo - de mi - neur L'a - mour vain -

queur _____ et la vie op - por - tu - ne,

Proses lyriques

1892-1893

I. De rêve

[1892-1893]

à V. Hocquet

poetry by Debussy

La nuit a des dou-ceurs de fem - me! Et les vieux ar - bres, sous la lu-ne d'or, Son - gent!

68

temps   où les é - pé - - - es   chan - taient ___ pour ___

El - - les!...

D'é - tran - ges sou - pirs   s'é - lè - vent sous les ar - bres.

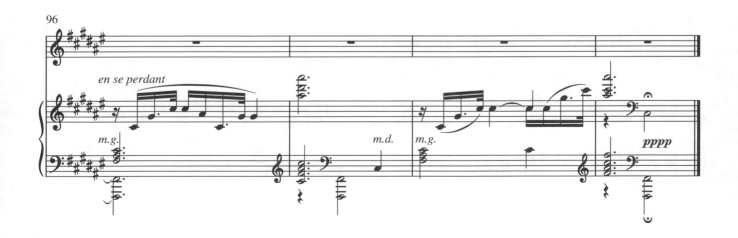

II. De grève

[1892-1893]

à Raymond Bonheur

poetry by Debussy

Modéré (mais sourdement agité)

pp très égal et très sourd

Sur la mer les cré - pus - cu - les tom - bent,

Soie blanche ef - fi - lé - e!

Les va – gues com-me de pe-ti-tes fol – les,

Ja – sent, pe-ti-tes fil-les sor – tant de l'é-col – le,

Par – mi les frou-frous de leur ro-be,

Soie verte i-ri-sé – e!

Les nu - a - ges, gra - ves vo - ya -

geurs, Se con - cer - tent sur le pro - chain o - ra - -

ge, Et c'est un fond vrai - ment trop gra - ve À cette an - glaise a - qua-

rel - le. Les va - gues,

les pe - ti - tes va - gues, Ne sa - vent plus où se met - tre,

Car voi - ci la mé - chante a - ver - se,

Frou - frous de ju - pes en - vo - lé - es,

Soie verte af - fo - lé - e.

42
res - se len - te - ment ses pe - ti - tes a -
44
mies, Qui s'of - frent com - me lè - vres ai -
3
46
pp
man - tes À ce tiède et
pp
48
Encore plus lent
blanc bai - ser. Puis,
pp

Plus rien!..._____ Plus que les clo - ches at - tar -

dé - es Des flot - tan - tes é - gli - ses!

plus p

An - gé - lus des va - gues,

plus pp

Soie blanche a - pai - sé - e!

ppp

très retenu

III. De fleurs

1893

à Madame E. Chausson

poetry by Debussy

Dans l'en-nui si dé-so-lé-ment vert De la
ser - re de dou-leur, Les Fleurs en-la - cent mon cœur De leurs ti - ges mé-
chan - tes. Ah! quand re - vien-dront au - tour de ma
tê - te Les chè - res mains si ten - dre - ment dé-sen-la - ceu - ses?

86

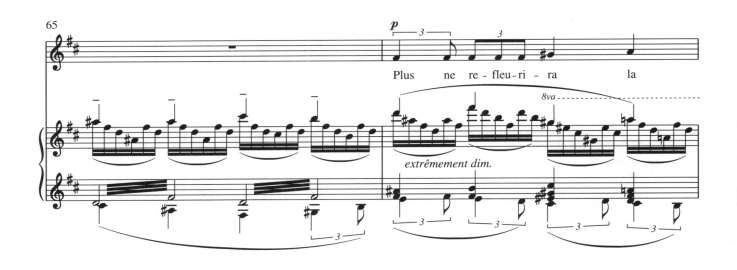

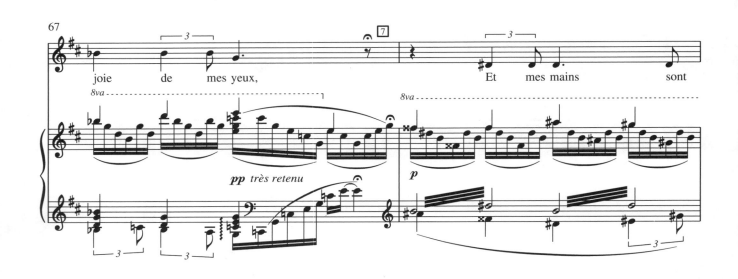

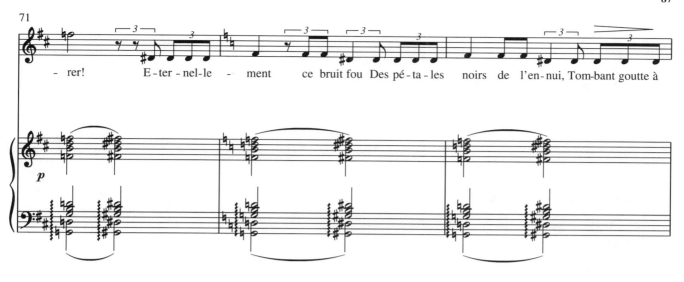

-rer! E-ter-nel-le - ment ce bruit fou Des pé-ta-les noirs de l'en-nui, Tom-bant goutte à

gout - te sur ma tê - te Dans le vert de la

ser - re de dou - leur!

IV. De soir

1893

à Henry Lerolle

poetry by Debussy

Di - man - che les trains vont vi - te, Dé - vo - rés par d'in - sa - ti - a - bles tun - nels; Et les bons si - gnaux des rou - tes É -

chan - gent d'un œil u - ni - que

Des im - pres - si - ons tou - tes mé - ca -

ni - ques.

dim.

plus diminué

Di - man - che,

Forts d'ab-so-lu-ti-on!

en se perdant

a tempo (plus lent)

Pre- nez pi-tié des vil - les,

Pre- nez pi-tié des cœurs, Vous, la Vier - ge

or sur ar - gent!

Trois chansons de Bilitis

1897 - 1898

I. La flûte de Pan

1897

Pierre Louÿs

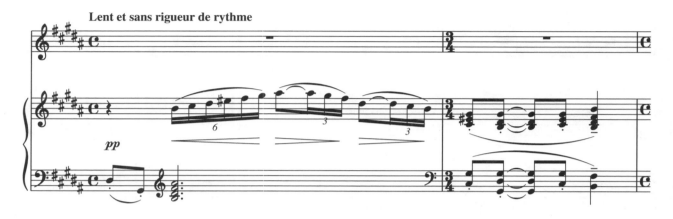

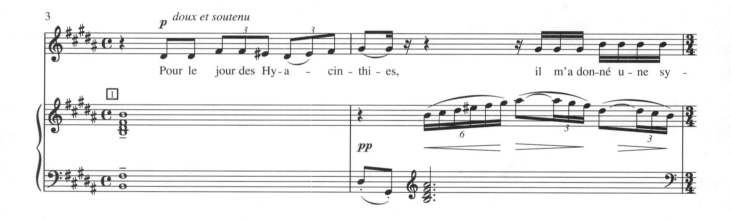

Pour le jour des Hy-a - cin-thi - es, il m'a don-né u - ne sy-

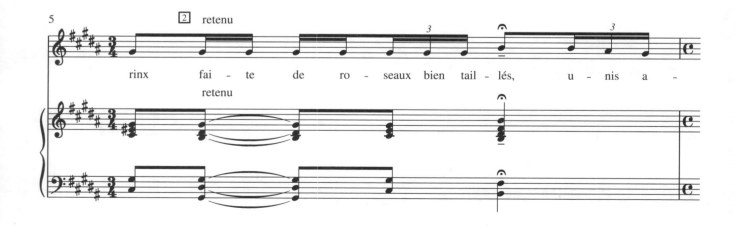

rinx fai - te de ro - seaux bien tail - lés, u - nis a -

rien à nous di - re, tant nous som-mes près l'un de l'autre; mais nos chan-

sons veu-lent se ré - pon-dre, et tour à tour nos bou - ches s'u - nis - sent sur la

flû - te.   Il est

tard;   voi-ci le chant des gre-nou-illes ver-tes qui com-

II. La chevelure

1897

Pierre Louÿs

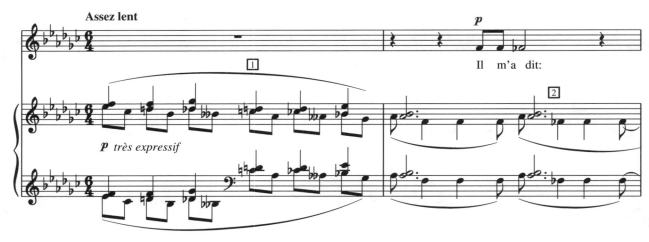

Il m'a dit:

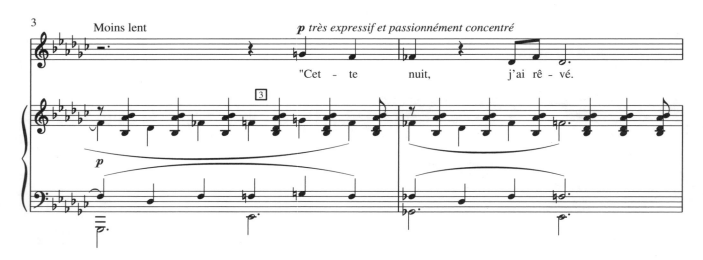

"Cet - te nuit, j'ai rê - vé.

J'a - vais ta che-ve - lure au-tour de mon cou.

par la mê-me che-ve-lu-re la bou-che sur la bou - che,

Tempo I

ain-si que deux lau-riers n'ont sou - vent qu'u-ne ra-ci - ne.

en pressant peu à peu et en augmentant

Et peu à peu, il m'a sem-blé, tant nos mem-bres é-

taient con-fon-dus, que je de-ve-nais toi-mê - me ou que tu en-trais en moi com-me mon

III. Le tombeau des Naïades

1898

dis ri - aient les Na - ïa - des.

Il pre - nait de grands mor - ceaux froids, et les sou - le - vant vers le ciel

pâle, il re - gar - dait au tra - vers.

retenu

Dans le jardin

1903

Paul Gravollet

Fêtes galantes, série II

1904

Dedicated to Emma Bardac

I. Les ingénus

Paul Verlaine

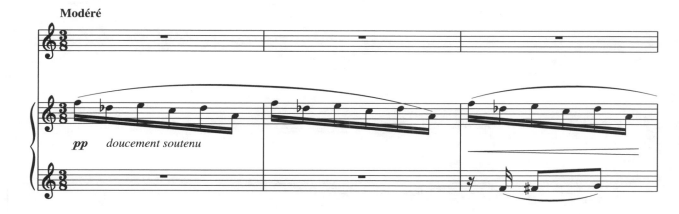

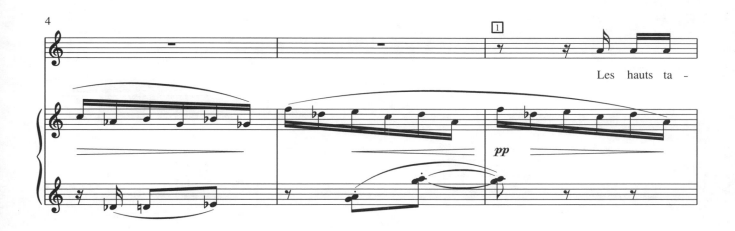

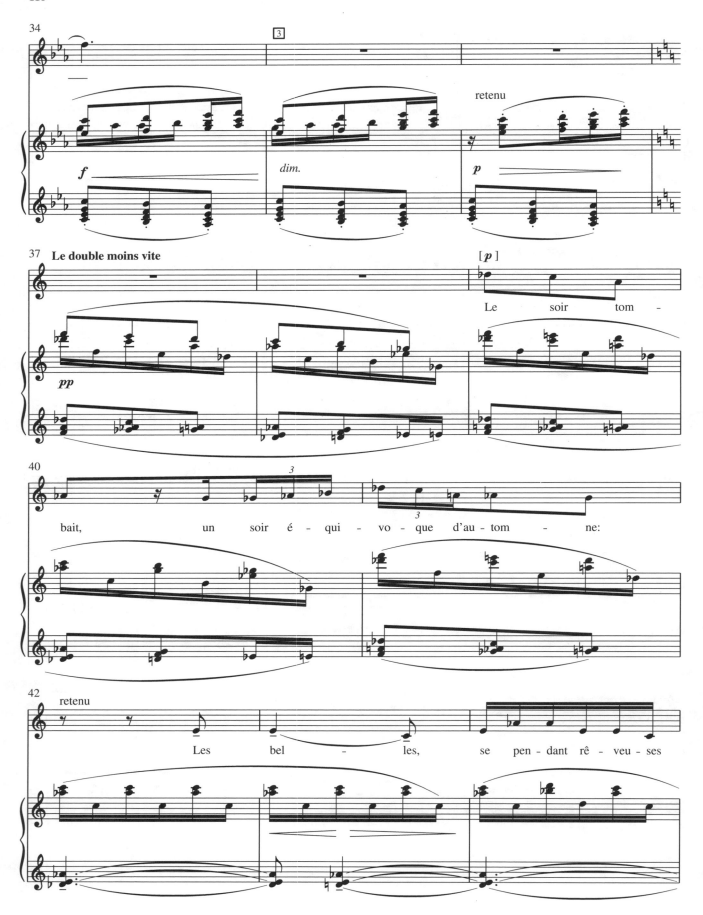

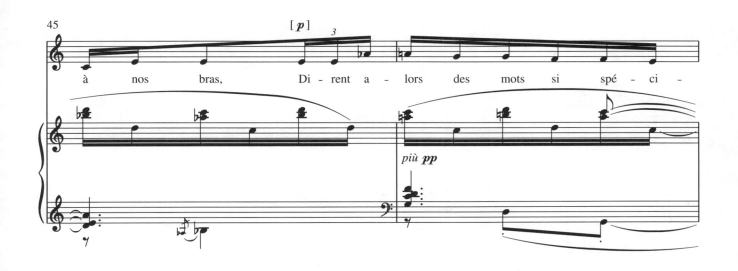

45

[*p*]

à nos bras, Di - rent a - lors des mots si spé - ci -

più pp

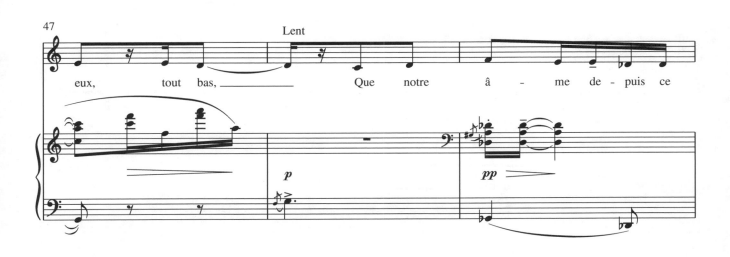

47

Lent

eux, tout bas, _____ Que notre â - me de - puis ce

p

pp

50

temps tremble et s'é - ton - ne.

m.g.

pp

più pp

ppp *sf* *pp*

II. Le faune

1904

Paul Verlaine

13

Un vieux fau- ne de ter- re

15

cui- te Rit au cen- tre des bou- lin- grins,____

pp

17

3

sf *p*

20

Pré- sa- geant sans doute u- ne sui- te Mau-

pp

heu - re dont la fui - te Tour -

noie au son des tam - bou - rins.

e perdendo

plus rien

III. Colloque sentimental

1904

Paul Verlaine

Triste et lent

Un peu plus mouvementé
Très expressif, mélancolique et lointain

—Te sou - vient - il de notre ex - tase an - cien - ne?

— Pour - quoi vou - lez - vous donc qu'il m'en sou - vien - ne?

—Ton cœur bat - il tou - jours à mon seul

29

nom? Tou - jours vois - tu mon âme en rê - ve?

pp

31

animez et augmentez peu à peu

— Non. —Ah!

p *p*

34

Les beaux jours de bon -

p e cresc. molto

36

heur in - di - ci - ble

8va

f *m.g.3*

38 retenu

Où nous joi-gnions nos bou-ches! — C'est pos-si-ble

a tempo

pp subito — *pp* — sempre *pp*

41

— Qu'il é-tait bleu, le ciel,

très expressif et soutenu

44

— et grand l'es-poir! — L'es-poir a fui, vain-

mf — *p*

47

cu, vers le ciel noir.

p — *p* — *più p*

retenu

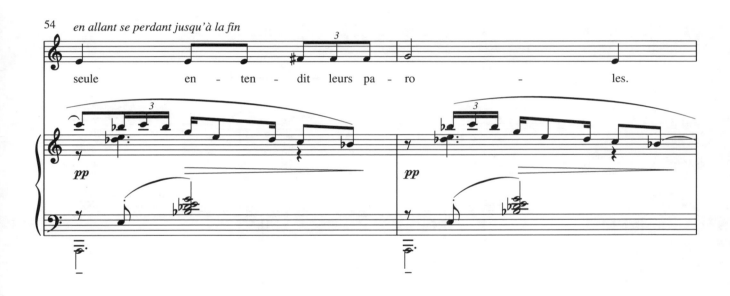

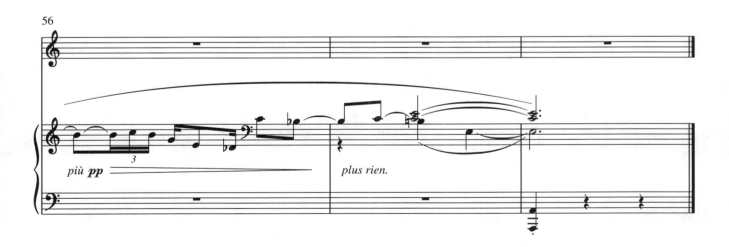

Trois chansons de France

1904

à Madame S. Bardac

I. Rondel ("Le temps")

Charles d'Orléans

viè - re,   fon - taine   et   ruis - seau

Por - tent, en li - vrée jo - ly - e,   Goul - tes d'ar - gent d'or - fa - ve -

ri - e.   Chas - cun s'a - bil - le de nou - veau,

Le   temps   a   lais - sié   son   man - teau.

II. La grotte

[1904]

Tristan Lhermite

Très lent et très doux

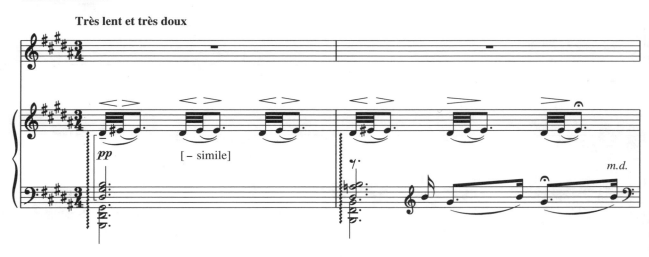

mière a - vec - que l'om - bre.

Ces flots, las - sés de l'ex - er - ci - ce Qu'ils ont

fait des - sus ce gra - vier, Se re - po - sent dans ce vi - vier

Un peu retenu

Où mou - rût au - tre - fois Nar - cis - se...

L'om - bre de cet - te fleur ver - meil - le
Et cel - le de ces joncs pen - dants
Pa - rais - sent
es - tre là de - dans
Les son - ges de l'eau qui som - meil - - le.

(la m.g. un peu en dehors)

III. Rondel ("Pour ce que Plaisance")

1904

Charles d'Orléans

Le temps ces nou-vel-les por - te Qui ne veut dé-duit a - voir;

Mais par for - ce du plou-voir Fait des champs clo-re la por - te, Pour ce que

Plai - sance est mor - te.

Le promenoir des deux amants

1910

à Emma Claude Debussy

I. La grotte (see above, number II in *Trois Chansons de France*)

II. Crois mon conseil, chère Climène

Tristan Lhermite

Crois mon con - seil, chè - re Cli - mè - ne;

Pour lais - ser ar - ri - ver le soir, Je te prie, al - lons nous as - seoir Sur le bord de cet - te fon -

III. Je tremble en voyant ton visage

1910

Tristan Lhermite

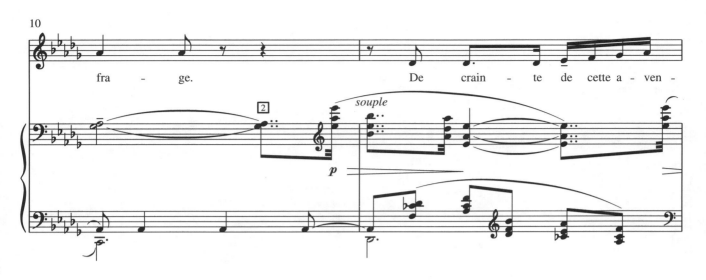

fra - ge.　De crain - te de cette a - ven -

tu - re Ne com-mets pas si li - bre-ment A cet in - fi - dèle___ é - lé - ment Tous les tré -

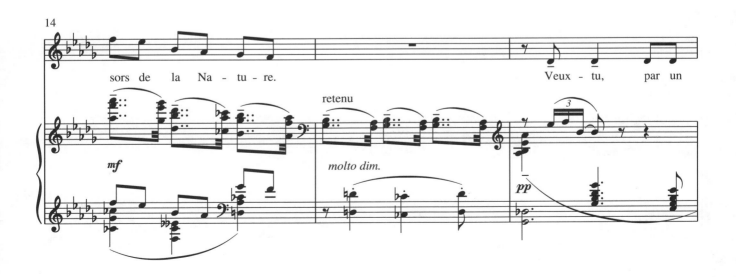

sors de la Na - tu - re.　Veux - tu, par un

17
doux pri - vi - lè - ge, Me mettre au - des - sus des hu - mains?

pp

20
Fais- moi boire au creux de tes mains, Si l'eau n'en dis - sout

retenu

pp

aussi doux que possible

23
point la nei - ge.

encore plus retenu

ppp

Trois ballades de François Villon

I. Ballade

de Villon à s'amye

1910

144

doux, mais appuyé

II. Ballade

que Villon feit à la requeste de sa mère
pour prier Nostre-Dame

1910

rir.　A　vos-tre　Filz　dic-tes　que　je　suys

sien-ne;　De　luy　soy-ent　mes　pe-chez a-bo-luz:　Par-don-nez-moy　comme à　l'E-gyp-ti-

En animant un peu

en – ne,　Ou　comme il　feit　au clerc The – o – phi – lus, Le-quel par vous fut quitte et ab-o-

luz,　Com-bien qu'il eust au dia – ble faict pro – mes-se.　Pre – ser-vez-moy　que je n'ac-com-plis-se

ce! Vier - ge por - tant sans rom-pure en-cou - rir Le sa - cre-ment qu'on ce - lebre à la mes - se.

En ces - te foy je vueil vivre et mou-rir. Fem - me je

suis po - vrette et an - ci - en - ne, Qui riens ne sçay; onc - ques let - tre ne

leuz; Au mou - stier voy dont suis pa - rois - si - en - ne, Pa - ra - dis painct où sont har - pes et

III. Ballade des femmes de Paris

1910

Quoy qu'on die _____ d'I - ta - li -

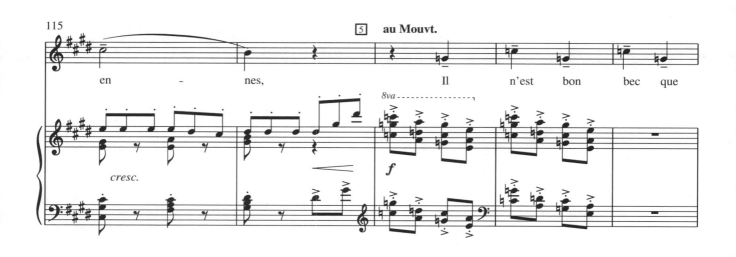

en - nes, Il n'est bon bec que

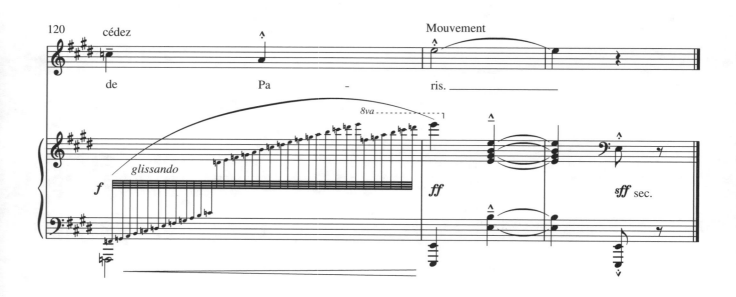

de Pa - ris. _____

Trois poèmes de Stéphane Mallarmé

1913

à la mémoire de Stéphane Mallarmé

I. Soupir

de ton œil an - gé - li - que Mon - te, com - me dans un jar - din mé - lan - co -

li - que, Fi - dè - le, un blanc jet d'eau sou - pi - re

en animant un peu

vers l'A - zur! Vers l'A - zur at - ten - dri d'Oc - to - bre pâle et

pur Qui mire aux grands bas - sins sa lan - gueur in - fi - nie Et lais - se, cédez

sur l'eau morte où la fauve a - go - nie Des feuil - les erre au vent et

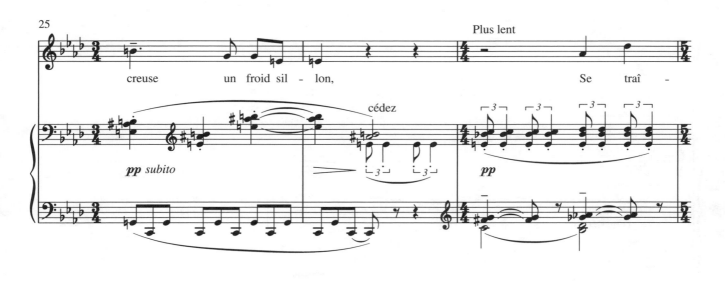

creuse un froid sil - lon, Se traî -

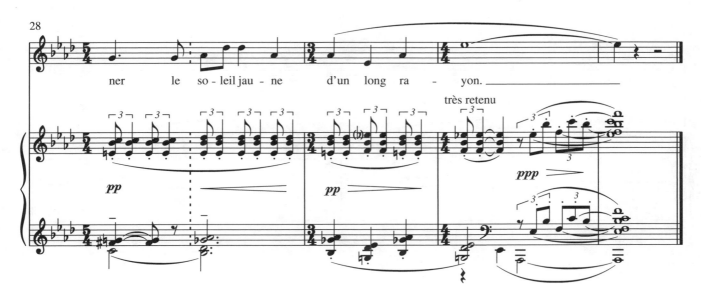

ner le so - leil jau - ne d'un long ra - yon. _____

II. Placet futile

1913

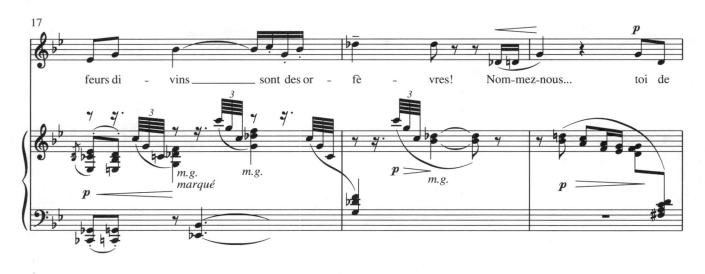

feurs di - vins ___ sont des or - fè - vres! Nom-mez-nous... toi de

qui tant de ris fram-boi-sés Se joi-gnent en trou-peau d'a-gneaux ap-pri-voi-

sés Chez tous brou-tant les vœux et bê - lant aux dé-li - res, Nom-mez-nous... pour qu'A-

mour ai - lé d'un é - ven - tail   M'y   pei - gne flûte aux doigts en - dor - mant ce ber-

sempre dolce

au Mouvt. un peu retardé

cail,   Prin - ces - se,   nom - mez-

molto dim.

nous   ber - ger de vous sou - ri   -   res.

pp

rapide et léger

III. Éventail

1913

Noël des enfants
qui n'ont plus de maisons

Text by Debussy

Glossary for Volume II

à peine — barely, subtly
a tempo — in the preceding regular tempo (before the rit. or other interruption)
à voix basse — in a low, quiet voice
accusé — in accusatory manner, sharply
agité — agitated, restless
ainsi qu'une flûte — as a flute
aise — ease; **à l'aise** — easily, with freedom
allant — moving. **Et en allant toujours se perdant** — and continuing to move while fading away in volume
animé (animato) — enliven in tempo (enlivened)
appuyé — leaned into
assez — quite
au mouvement — as **a tempo**
augmentant — increasing
avec une douceur triste — with a sad quietness
avec une expression sourde — with muffled expression
calmant — calming
caressant — caressing, gently
cédez — yield, slow down the tempo slightly
dans le mouvt. d'un menuet lent — in the tempo of a slow minuet
dehors — played out, projected
diminué — diminished in volume
dolent — sad
double plus lent, double moins vite — twice as slowly
doux, doucement — quiet, gentle
extrêmement — extremely
gai, gaiment — gay, gaily
intimement — intimately
joyeux, joyeusement — joyous, joyously
las — weary, sluggish
léger — light, delicate
lent, lentement — slow, slowly
lointain — far away. **Très lointain, sans nuances mais pourtant bien rythmé** — very far away,
without nuance but still quite rhythmic
mais — but
marqué — marked, emphasized
mélancolique — melancholy
même mouvt. — in the same tempo
meno — less
modéré — moderate tempo
moins — less
moqueur — mocking
mouvement — tempo (as **a tempo)**
murmuré — in a whisper, murmured
pénétrant — with penetrating expression
perdant, perdendo — dying away in sound
peu — little; **un peu** — a little; **peu à peu** — gradually
pieusement — piously
più, plus — more
poco a poco – gradually
poco più lento — a little more slowly
premier mouvement — in the tempo of the beginning
pressez, en pressant — press, pressing ahead
primo tempo (I° tempo) — as premier mouvement
progressivement — progressively, steadily
recueilli — gathered in, withheld

retardé — held back in tempo
retenant (retenu) — holding back (held back)
revenez — return
rêveusement — dreamily
sans dureté — without harshness
sans rigueur de rythme — without rigorous rhythm
serrant, serrez — pressing, pressed ahead
souple — supple
sourd, sourdement — deafenned, muffled
soutenu — sustained
toujours — always, still
très — very
triste, tristement — sad, sadly
vif — lively
vite — quickly